India's Industrial Odyssey

India's Industrial Odyssey

Steel, Power, Progress

Olivia K

UNIEK ENTERPRISES

CONTENTS

Chapter 7: "Entrepreneurial Spirit: Success Stories and Challenges"
7.1 Profiles of successful Indian entrepreneurs
7.2 Challenges faced by entrepreneurs in a competitive global market
7.3 The spirit of Indian entrepreneurship

Introduction

In the huge and perplexing woven artwork of mankind's set of experiences, certain ages stand apart as extraordinary minutes that have modified the direction of countries and social orders. India's modern process is one such section in the stupendous account of human advancement. This multi-layered odyssey is a demonstration of the country's versatility, desire, and flexibility. From the cinders of provincial oppression to the lively tints of post-autonomy progress, India's modern advancement has been completely exceptional.

At the core of this account is the metallurgical wonder known as steel. The manufacturing of steel and the saddling of force have been the twin motors moving India into the cutting edge period. Steel, with its surprising strength and flexibility, has been the foundation of framework, and power, in its different structures, has stimulated the country's development. Together, they have gotten the wheels of progress under way, rethinking India's put on the worldwide stage.

The modern adventure of India is inseparably connected with its pioneer history. The English Domain, with its unquenchable hunger for unrefined components and markets, saw India as a mother lode of assets. Notwithstanding, for a large part of the pilgrim time frame, India's modern ability was smothered, and its possible lay torpid, oppressed under the heaviness of dominion. However, even in the most obscure hours, ashes of industry kept on sparkling. India's battle for autonomy was set apart by the longing for political sway as well as for monetary independence.

The introduction of India as a free country in 1947 proclaimed another sunrise in its modern process. A recently free India was anxious to recover its legitimate spot on the planet, not as a compliant state but rather as a confident, self-supporting country. The post-autonomy time acquired with it an uncommon flood modern development. The steel business, specifically, expected a focal job in this change.

The ascent of steel in India was not only an issue of monetary turn of events; it was an image of public pride and character. Steel, with its unyielding strength and pliability, turned into a similitude for India's versatility and flexibility. The underlying foundations of India's steel industry can be followed back to the pre-freedom period, with a couple of limited scope units delivering iron and steel. Nonetheless, it wasn't long after autonomy that the business really started to thrive.

The foundation of public-area steel plants, similar to the Bhilai Steel Plant and Bokaro Steel Plant, denoted a huge defining moment in India's modern scene. These uber projects were not just about creating steel; they were about country building. They addressed the goals of a youthful, autonomous India, anxious to break liberated from the shackles of the past and cut its own predetermination. The development of these plants was a designing wonder, a demonstration of India's designing and administrative capacities.

The excursion of India's steel industry was not without challenges. From innovative bottlenecks to monetary limitations, the way was filled with hindrances. Nonetheless, it was the enduring soul of development and assurance that permitted India to beat these obstacles. The reception of present day advancements and worldwide coordinated efforts assumed an essential part in the development of the steel area. The Green Upheaval, driven by mechanical headways and an emphasis on independence, was instrumental in molding the modern scene.

While the steel business arose as an image of India's modern ability, power age was similarly crucial in catalyzing progress. Energy has been the soul of industrialization, and India's excursion in this domain has been similarly astounding. The country's power area went through critical changes, moving from an overwhelmingly agrarian and provincial society to an additional urbanized and industrialized one.

The foundation of the Public Nuclear energy Company (NTPC) in 1975 denoted a huge jump in India's power age limit. NTPC turned into a crucial player in the improvement of the nation's power area, cultivating a culture of confidence and energy security. The progression of the Indian economy during the 1990s further opened the entryways for private support in the power area, prompting a broadening of force age sources.

As India flooded forward in the modern circle, the energy area was pushed by a double spotlight on coal and environmentally friendly power. The coal area, long a foundation of India's power age, went through modernization and extension. The presentation of cleaner innovations and a pledge to diminishing ecological effect prompted the improvement of supercritical and super supercritical coal-based power plants.

In equal, India set out on an excursion to bridle the colossal capability of environmentally friendly power sources. Sun oriented and wind power have arisen as critical supporters of the country's energy blend. Drives like the Public Sun oriented Mission and wind energy projects have changed the scene, making India a worldwide forerunner in sustainable power reception.

The concurrence of customary and current power age strategies mirrors India's logical way to deal with energy security. As the country tries to adjust the requests of monetary development and natural maintainability, it has exhibited a pledge to embracing cleaner and more practical wellsprings of force while recognizing the significance of coal in guaranteeing energy security.

The advancement in India's steel and power areas has been naturally connected to the country's more extensive financial change. The 1991 financial changes, frequently alluded to as the "New Monetary Strategy," were a turning point in India's set of experiences. These changes opened up the Indian economy to globalization and progression, introducing a period of more prominent financial reconciliation with the worldwide local area.

The steel and power areas were not safe to the undeniable trends achieved by advancement. Unfamiliar direct venture (FDI) streamed into the nation, prompting expanded support of global organizations in India's modern scene.

In the resulting years, the development of these areas reflected the generally financial advancement of the country. The development of foundation, the ascent of the working class, and the launch of new business sectors added to the consistently expanding interest for steel and power. This developing hunger for modern items energized further speculations and advancement in the particular areas.

The steel business, specifically, assumed an essential part in India's framework improvement. The development of parkways, scaffolds, air terminals, and structures requested immense amounts of steel. The development of the car area, with India arising as one of the world's biggest auto makers, was one more critical driver of steel interest. The steel business answered these requests with modernization, development, and an emphasis on quality and effectiveness.

India's power area, then again, wrestled with the test of meeting the energy needs of a quickly urbanizing and industrializing country. The interest for power was voracious, and the power area needed to stay up with the thriving requirements of both metropolitan and rustic populaces. The public authority presented drives, for example, the "Power for All" program to guarantee all inclusive admittance to power.

In this journey for energy security, India likewise found a way aggressive ways to outfit the capability of thermal power. The atomic area, while full of worldwide administrative difficulties, held guarantee for perfect and manageable power age. The development of thermal energy stations, joint efforts with worldwide accomplices, and an emphasis on wellbeing and security have been key drivers of India's atomic power desires.

In the midst of these astounding turns of events, the difficulties of manageability, ecological effect, and social obligation have acquired unmistakable quality. The steel and power areas have wrestled with issues of ecological contamination, land securing, and removal of networks. Supportable and mindful practices are presently not only discretionary however basic for the proceeded with development of these enterprises.

The reception of cleaner innovations, the advancement of sustainable power, and the accentuation on corporate social obligation have become basic to the modern scene. These businesses are currently taken part in a difficult exercise, endeavoring to fulfill the needs of financial development while limiting their environmental impression and adding to the social government assistance of the networks they work in.

The tale of India's modern odyssey isn't only about numbers and measurements; it is about the lives and yearnings of millions of people. The development of the steel and power areas has set out positions and monetary open doors as well as achieved a change in the personal satisfaction for some. As enterprises have extended, they have frequently turned into the central marks of provincial turn of events, cultivating development in adjacent regions and further developing framework and expectations for everyday comforts.

Training and ability advancement have been fundamental parts of this change. As the interest for talented work has developed, the steel and power businesses have put resources into preparing and ability upgrade projects to outfit the labor force with the essential apparatuses and information. The strengthening of the labor force, particularly in country regions, has been a critical social advantage of modern development.

Moreover, the modern excursion has not been bound to a specific locale or gathering. The advantages and open doors made by these areas have arrived at all over, contacting metropolitan and provincial India the same. The steel and power enterprises have been instrumental in lessening provincial differences and advancing comprehensive development.

Chapter 1

"The Birth of Industry"

The beginning of the modern age denoted a vital crossroads in mankind's set of experiences, reshaping the manner in which social orders worked, economies worked, and daily routines were experienced. The introduction of industry released a rush of development and change that cleared across the globe, everlastingly modifying the direction of human advancement. This significant shift from agrarian economies to modern ones had extensive results, contacting each feature of life and making ready for advancement as far as we might be concerned.

The progress from agrarian social orders to modern forces to be reckoned with was a continuous cycle, set apart by a progression of interconnected improvements that traversed hundreds of years. The seeds of industry were planted in pre-modern Europe, where a conjunction of variables gave fruitful ground to development and monetary development. Agribusiness, the foundation of pre-modern economies, started to advance through developments like yield turn and worked on cultivating procedures. These advances prompted expanded food creation, diminished starvation, and, thusly, a developing populace.

The development in populace applied strain on existing financial frameworks. Feudalism, the predominant social and financial design, started to give indications of strain as the populace blossomed. Land became more difficult to find, and the conventional agrarian framework couldn't oblige the growing workforce. This segment shift required an adjustment of the manner in which individuals worked and lived.

At the same time, progressions in innovation and logical comprehension gave the devices and information required for the modern transformation to flourish. The creation of the turning jenny, the flying transport, and other material hardware in the eighteenth century upset the material business, empowering large scale manufacturing of materials and making way for industrialization. Besides, forward leaps in energy age, especially with the improvement of the steam motor, considered the automation of plants and changed how products were made.

The Modern Upheaval was not an unexpected occasion but instead an extended cycle that unfurled more than a very long while. Its starting points can be followed back to the late eighteenth hundred years in Britain, where the union of various variables pushed the change. The material business, one of the essential drivers of industrialization, went through a huge transformation. Plants arose, fueled by steam motors, and they introduced another time of large scale manufacturing.

The motorization of material assembling was only the start. Before long, different businesses stuck to this same pattern, taking on machines and innovation to upgrade efficiency. Iron and coal mining, both indispensable assets for industry, experienced quick development. The development of trenches and, later, rail lines worked with the transportation of merchandise and unrefined substances, further empowering modern extension. These mechanical advancements were not restricted to the material and transportation areas. Steam-controlled machines and motors tracked down applications in different enterprises, including mining, assembling, and farming.

One of the most groundbreaking parts of the Modern Upset was the progress from hand creation to machine-based assembling. The production line framework arose, prompting a huge change in labor rehearses. Laborers who once created items by hand wound up working machines inside the limits of a manufacturing plant, dependent upon the rhythms of modern creation. This adjustment of work elements had significant ramifications for the workforce and society at large.

As processing plants multiplied and metropolitan focuses extended, a huge movement from country regions to urban communities happened. This movement, frequently alluded to as urbanization, was driven by the commitment of work in prospering businesses. Individuals ran to the modern habitats, looking for better financial possibilities, regardless of the frequently horrid everyday environments and long working hours that looked for them. The modern cityscape was a distinct difference to the provincial, agrarian scenes of the past.

The social outcomes of this shift were critical. Customary agrarian networks were upset as families got away from genealogical grounds to work in processing plants. The nuclear family itself went through change, as production line work forced an unbending division among work and home life, with brief period left for relaxation or public exercises. By and large, youngster work turned into a need, as whole families were brought into the modern workforce.

While industrialization achieved various social difficulties, it additionally offered open doors for cultural advancement. The development of manufacturing plants prompted an expansion sought after for gifted work. As laborers acquired insight and particular information, they looked for better working circumstances and higher wages. Trade guilds and specialist developments started to arise as a reaction to the frequently brutal and shady circumstances in production lines.

The monetary scene additionally saw significant changes. Free enterprise, the monetary framework in light of private responsibility for method for creation and a benefit driven ethos, turned out to be progressively conspicuous. The ascent of entrepreneur ventures, powered by industrialization, presented new financial elements. Business people put resources into production lines and apparatus, procuring benefits from the work of modern specialists. This monetary framework prompted the improvement of a market-driven economy, where market interest decided costs and creation levels.

Industrialization changed the actual embodiment of work, testing laid out standards and assumptions. In the pre-modern period, work was frequently attached to a provincial scene, where occasional farming exercises directed the mood of life. With the appearance of industry, work became separated from regular rhythms, as production lines worked nonstop. The customary examples of agrarian life were supplanted by the persistent beat of machines and mechanical production systems.

Notwithstanding the troubles and difficulties related with the beginning stages of industrialization, it introduced an influx of development and progress. The efficiency gains from automation and the large scale manufacturing of merchandise prompted an expansion in the accessibility of items and the improvement of expectations for everyday comforts for some. Manufacturing plant made merchandise turned out to be more reasonable and open, making regular things, when thought about extravagances, accessible to a more extensive area of the populace.

The improvement of transportation organizations, especially the extension of rail lines, further changed the development of individuals and merchandise. This considered the more extensive conveyance of items and admittance to new business sectors. Thus, a worldwide economy started to come to fruition, with the development of unrefined components, completed products, and even individuals advancing at a phenomenal speed. The Modern Upset spanned holes and made interconnected networks that changed the world's financial and social texture.

The development of industry significantly affected the design of society. Another working class arose, contained business people, industrialists, and experts who assumed urgent parts in the modern economy. This social layer, frequently portrayed by up portability, used expanding impact and abundance. The customary differentiations between friendly classes started to obscure, as industrialization set out open doors for people to work on their social and monetary standing.

The Modern Upheaval didn't just rethink the social and monetary scene; it likewise altered logical and mechanical progressions. Advancements in hardware, materials, and assembling processes impelled society into a period of remarkable logical advancement. Specialists and designers like James Watt, Eli Whitney, and Samuel Morse made historic commitments that altered enterprises and correspondence. The Modern Insurgency, with its intrinsic spotlight on advancement and productivity, laid the foundation for resulting logical and innovative leap forwards.

As industry extended and advertises developed, the world turned out to be more interconnected than any other time. The Modern Unrest was not restricted to a solitary country or locale; its effect reverberated universally. Europe, especially Britain, filled in as the focal point of the industrialization wave, yet the impacts undulated across mainlands. The US, for example, encountered its own modern upheaval, portrayed by the development of manufacturing plants, urbanization, and mechanical advancement.

In different regions of the planet, the Modern Upheaval put into high gear a progression of financial and social changes. Provincial powers incorporated their settlements into the worldwide economy, separating assets and work to fuel their modern motors. The outcomes of this mix, including financial differences, keep on forming worldwide elements.

Be that as it may, the advantages of industry didn't arrive at everybody similarly. The newly discovered riches and flourishing were much of the time gathered in the possession of a couple, leaving numerous in destitution and filth. While industrialization prodded advancement and monetary development, it additionally achieved critical social and ecological difficulties. Metropolitan ghettos and unfortunate working circumstances were a typical sight in modern habitats, and the cost for the climate was obvious in contamination and asset exhaustion.

Industrialization, regardless of its groundbreaking power, was not without its faultfinders. Essayists, masterminds, and activists, like Karl Marx, Charles Dickens, and Friedrich Engels, featured the situation of the common laborers and the disparities propagated by entrepreneur frameworks. Work developments and laborers' freedoms drives picked up speed as the modern labor force looked for better circumstances and impartial treatment.

The late nineteenth 100 years and the mid twentieth century saw a progression of work changes and lawful securities pointed toward tending to the social and monetary difficulties presented by industrialization. Regulations were instituted to manage working circumstances.

1.1 Early industrial efforts in pre-independence India

The account of industrialization in India is one of versatility, advancement, and variation. Some time before acquiring freedom in 1947, India left on an excursion to set up a good foundation for itself as a modern force to be reckoned with. While frequently eclipsed by the modern upheavals in the Western world, India's initial modern endeavors were set apart by critical accomplishments and difficulties, mirroring a country taking a stab at financial independence and progress.

The pre-freedom time frame in India was described by a dominatingly agrarian economy. Most of the populace relied upon agribusiness for their jobs, and the modern area was in its beginning stages. The Indian economy was basically agrarian, and a significant part of the modern movement was gathered in conventional areas like materials, crafted works, and metalwork. In any case, there was a developing acknowledgment of the requirement for financial enhancement and the foundation of a vigorous modern base.

One of the earliest areas to see modern endeavors in pre-freedom India was materials. India had a rich custom of material creation going back hundreds of years, known for its complicated plans and quality textures. The presentation of current innovation and apparatus could change the material business and increment creation productivity. This was especially huge given the worldwide interest for Indian materials.

In the mid nineteenth hundred years, the English pioneer organization started to present automated turning and winding in India. The foundation of force looms, alongside the import of current material hardware, denoted the start of automated material creation. This shift had significant ramifications for the conventional handloom weavers, who confronted contest from the automated area.

The material business in India was additionally impacted by the establishing of the main material plant in Bombay (presently Mumbai) in 1854 by Cowasji Davar. This noticeable a critical achievement in India's modern history, as it was the principal case of a material plant being set up with current hardware. The factory used steam power and present day gear to create cotton materials, an area that would later turn into a foundation of India's modern scene.

One more critical second in the early industrialization of India was the foundation of the Indian Rail routes. The presentation of rail lines was a distinct advantage, as it essentially further developed transportation and network. The first traveler train in Quite a while ran from Bombay to Thane in 1853, and this obvious the start of a broad rail route network that worked with the development of products and individuals the nation over.

The improvement of rail routes had sweeping consequences for India's modern scene. It made the transportation of unrefined substances, completed items, and work more proficient, working with the development of ventures in different areas. It additionally added to the improvement of mining and weighty ventures as the rail routes made the foundation expected to move unrefined substances like coal and iron mineral.

While early industrialization endeavors in India were picking up speed, they confronted moves that went from mechanical restrictions to financial limitations. The absence of a homegrown hardware industry implied that modern gear and apparatus must be imported, which presented difficulties with regards to cost and support. Also, the English provincial organization inclined toward the English assembling industry, prompting arrangements that prevented the development of native ventures.

The monetary circumstance in pre-freedom India was likewise portrayed by restricted capital and admittance to credit. The development of enterprises required significant speculation, which was much of the time past the method for Indian business people. The absence of admittance to credit and fund restricted the capacity of Indian business visionaries to put resources into hardware, framework, and gifted work.

Notwithstanding these difficulties, early modern endeavors in pre-freedom India were driven by a dream of confidence and financial advancement. Business visionaries like Jamsetji Goodbye assumed a critical part in India's modern turn of events. In 1907, Goodbye laid out the Goodbye Iron and Steel Organization (presently Goodbye

Steel) in Jamshedpur, denoting a critical stage in the improvement of the steel business in India.

Goodbye's vision was not restricted to the steel business; he additionally established Goodbye Power in 1911, perceiving the significance of power in the industrialization cycle. The foundation of Goodbye Steel and Goodbye Power addressed a defining moment in India's modern process, as these organizations set up for the development of weighty ventures and framework improvement.

One more striking figure in India's initial industrialization was Ardeshir Godrej, who, alongside his sibling Pirojsha, established the Godrej Gathering in 1897. The Godrej Gathering at first began as a lock producing organization yet before long enhanced into different areas, including shopper merchandise, synthetics, and machines. The Godrej Gathering's obligation to quality and development established the groundwork for its future progress in the Indian market.

The early industrialization endeavors in pre-freedom India were not exclusively determined by the confidential area. The pilgrim government additionally perceived the requirement for modern turn of events and laid out a few public-area endeavors. The foundation of endeavors like the Indian Rail routes, the Indian Posts and Broadcasts, and the Indian Mandate Manufacturing plants was a demonstration of the public authority's job in advancing industrialization.

In any case, it's fundamental to recognize that the industrialization endeavors during the pioneer time frame were principally arranged towards serving English monetary interests. The pilgrim organization frequently deterred the improvement of enterprises that might actually rival English businesses. This prompted a huge lopsidedness in the modern scene, where India fundamentally filled in as a wellspring of unrefined substances and a business opportunity for English fabricated products.

The segment of Bengal in 1905 was a critical crossroads in India's pre-freedom history and had suggestions for industrialization. The parcel was met with far and wide fights and resistance, and it was in the long run turned around in 1911. This occasion exhibited the political and social age of the time and featured the job of neighborhood pioneers and networks in molding the course of India's set of experiences.

WWI (1914-1918) significantly affected India's initial industrialization endeavors. The conflict spurred a flood in interest for different items, prompting an expansion in modern creation. Indian enterprises were prepared to help the conflict exertion, and this period saw a brief lift in assembling and monetary movement. Be that as it may, it additionally uncovered the constraints of India's modern framework, as the nation was vigorously dependent on imports for apparatus and hardware.

The post-The Second Great War time frame saw the continuation of industrialization endeavors in India. The development of native enterprises picked up speed, and business people like Walchand Hirachand assumed a pivotal part in the improvement of India's flying industry. In 1928, Walchand laid out the Hindustan Airplane Restricted, later known as Hindustan Flying Restricted (HAL). This undeniable India's introduction to airplane fabricating and established the groundwork for the flying area's development.

The 1930s saw the development of the auto business in India, with the foundation of the Hindustan Engine Assembling Organization in 1942. This undeniable the start of the Indian auto industry, which would later become one of the nation's critical modern areas. The car business assumed a huge part in forming India's cutting edge modern scene.

Notwithstanding the different modern endeavors in pre-freedom India, the economy remained vigorously agrarian. The majority of the populace was participated in agribusiness, and industrialization was still in its beginning phases. The difficulties of insufficient framework, absence of capital, and restricted admittance to innovation kept on frustrating the development of businesses.

The Economic crisis of the early 20s of the 1930s had a worldwide effect, remembering for India. The financial slump prompted a decrease in modern creation and brought about boundless joblessness. It further highlighted the requirement for financial broadening and the improvement of a more powerful modern base.

As the pre-freedom time frame attracted to a nearby, the industrialization endeavors in India had established a groundwork for future development and improvement. The foundation of organizations like Goodbye Steel, Hindustan Engine, and Hindustan Flying, among others, checked huge achievements in the country's modern process. These early modern trailblazers set up for the development and enhancement of India's modern scene in the post-freedom time.

It's vital to perceive that the pre-freedom period in India was set apart by a mind boggling exchange of frontier strategies, enterprising soul, and social and monetary difficulties. While industrialization endeavors confronted various deterrents, they mirrored a country's yearning for confidence, monetary advancement, and a more different and energetic modern scene.

The early industrialization endeavors in pre-freedom India addressed a part in the country's set of experiences when the seeds of industry were planted. The difficulties and accomplishments of this period laid the basis for the post-freedom modern development that would push India into another time of monetary turn of events and independence. The tale of pre-freedom industrialization is a demonstration of the flexibility and vision of a country that tried to shape its fate in a quickly impacting world.

1.2 The role of key pioneers and visionaries

Since forever ago, the turn of events and development of enterprises have been essentially affected by visionary people whose creative thoughts and spearheading endeavors have left an enduring effect. From the beginning phases of industrialization to the current day, these critical trailblazers and visionaries play had an instrumental impact in forming businesses, driving development, and changing social orders.

During the Modern Transformation, a period set apart by mechanical progressions and the ascent of motorized creation, a few eminent figures arose as trailblazers in different fields. One such figure was James Watt, whose enhancements to the steam motor were an impetus for modern advancement. Watt's creative changes to the steam motor, for example, the different condenser, enormously improved its productivity and common sense, prompting its far reaching reception in enterprises going from materials to mining.

In the material business, Richard Arkwright, frequently alluded to as the "Father of the Modern Upset," made huge commitments. Arkwright's creation of the water outline, a turning machine fueled by water, changed the material assembling process. This development changed the material business by empowering large scale manufacturing, expanding productivity, and laying the basis for the processing plant framework.

The transportation area likewise saw the impact of key trailblazers. George Stephenson, known as the "Father of Rail routes," made critical commitments to the improvement of the rail route framework. Stephenson's formation of the world's most memorable commonsense steam train, the "Rocket," assumed a significant part in laying out present day rail transport. His designing ability and inventive plans moved the extension of rail organizations, changing transportation and exchange.

In the beginning phases of India's industrialization, a few critical trailblazers and visionaries assumed an essential part in establishing the groundwork for the country's modern development. One of the most conspicuous figures was Jamsetji Goodbye, a visionary industrialist who established the Goodbye Gathering. Goodbye's commitments to the Indian modern scene were multi-layered. He laid out the Goodbye Iron and Steel Organization (presently Goodbye Steel) in 1907, India's previously coordinated steel plant. His vision and assurance laid the basis for the development of the steel business in India.

Goodbye's impact stretched out past steel. He additionally established Goodbye Power in 1911, perceiving the significance of electrical power in modern turn of events. These undertakings highlighted Goodbye's obligation to laying out fundamental framework for India's modern development. His vision, combined with a promise to mechanical headway and social government assistance, established the groundwork for the Goodbye Gathering's expanded modern presence in India.

One more critical figure in India's modern history was Ardeshir Godrej, the fellow benefactor of the Godrej Gathering. Godrej's spearheading endeavors in the late nineteenth hundred years in lock producing prepared for the gathering's venture into different enterprises, including shopper products, machines, and synthetic substances. His accentuation on quality and development set the vibe for the Godrej Gathering's future progress in the Indian market.

Besides, industrialists like Walchand Hirachand made critical commitments to India's initial avionics industry. Hirachand's foundation of Hindustan Airplane Restricted (later known as Hindustan Air transportation Restricted) in 1928 denoted

India's entrance into airplane fabricating. His spearheading endeavors laid the foundation for the development of the flight area and the improvement of native aviation abilities.

The car area in India likewise saw the impact of key trailblazers. The foundation of the Hindustan Engine Assembling Organization in 1942 denoted the start of the Indian car industry. The spearheading endeavors of these visionaries set up for the improvement of a powerful car area, which would later become one of the country's essential modern portions.

In the domain of innovation and data, people like Bill Doors and Steve Occupations play played groundbreaking parts in molding the scene of the advanced tech industry. Charge Entryways, the fellow benefactor of Microsoft, assumed a vital part in carrying individualized computing to the majority. His vision of putting a PC in each home and office made ready for the computerized transformation. Microsoft's working frameworks and programming became indispensable to the advancement of figuring.

Steve Occupations, the prime supporter of Mac Inc., was one more visionary whose effect on the tech business couldn't possibly be more significant. Occupations' steady quest for development and plan greatness prompted the making of famous items like the iPhone, iPad, and Mac PCs. His accentuation on client experience and stylish allure reformed shopper hardware and affected plan patterns across businesses.

Elon Musk, known for his pivotal endeavors in different areas, has been a main thrust in enterprises going from electric vehicles to space investigation. Musk's establishing of organizations like Tesla, SpaceX, and Neuralink has altogether affected the auto, aviation, and innovation areas. His vision for reasonable energy and human colonization of Mars has impelled innovative headways and re-imagined industry norms.

In the field of environmentally friendly power, figures like Elon Musk and heads of organizations like Tesla have been at the bleeding edge of propelling clean energy advances. The quest for sunlight based power, wind energy, and other economical arrangements has picked up speed, driven by the visionaries expecting to lessen dependence on petroleum derivatives and alleviate environmental change.

The job of trailblazers and visionaries in the drug business has been similarly persuasive. People like Alexander Fleming, the pioneer of penicillin, and Jonas Salk, the engineer of the polio immunization, have made historic commitments that upset medical care. Their revelations and advancements in medication have saved endless lives and made way for present day drug innovative work.

Visionaries in the field of social business and corporate social obligation have likewise had a tremendous effect. Figures like Muhammad Yunus, the pioneer behind Grameen Bank and a Nobel Harmony Prize laureate, have supported microfinance and social plans of action pointed toward easing neediness and engaging networks. Their obligation to social change and feasible improvement has impacted the corporate scene, cultivating a more prominent accentuation on moral and socially mindful strategic policies.

In addition, the job of key trailblazers and visionaries in ecological preservation and supportability can't be neglected. Figures like Wangari Maathai, the pioneer behind the Green Belt Development, and Al Carnage, a noticeable natural promoter, have been instrumental in bringing issues to light about ecological issues and supporting for preservation endeavors. Their work has affected public arrangement, corporate practices, and cultural mentalities toward natural stewardship.

The effect of these critical trailblazers and visionaries rises above individual ventures. Their commitments have prompted extraordinary headways, reshaped business ideal models, and catalyzed cultural changes. Their creative reasoning, versatility, and assurance have driven innovative advancement as well as affected social standards, cultural qualities, and moral norms inside ventures.

The meaning of trailblazers and visionaries stretches out past their nearby accomplishments; it lies in their capacity to imagine conceivable outcomes, drive change, and motivate others. These people have gone about as impetuses for development and progress, leaving a significant and persevering through heritage in their particular fields. Their commitments have molded enterprises as well as affected the more extensive structure holding the system together, setting benchmarks for people in the future and filling in as directing lights for advancement and progress.

1.3 The influence of the independence movement on industrialization

The battle for freedom in numerous nations has been a mind boggling and multi-layered process, described by political, social, and financial changes. In India, the mission for independence from English pilgrim rule was inseparably connected to the country's financial turn of events and industrialization. The impact of the freedom development on industrialization in India was significant, as it reshaped the country's financial scene, strategies, and needs.

The underlying foundations of the Indian freedom development can be followed back to the nineteenth century when a feeling of public character started to arise. This period saw the ascent of pioneers like Raja Smash Mohan Roy, who upheld for social and instructive changes. The Indian Public Congress, established in 1885, turned into a critical political stage for articulating the goals of a country looking for self-administration.

One of the earliest financial results of the freedom development was the rise of Swadeshi, a development that intended to advance native ventures and blacklist unfamiliar products. Swadeshi called for confidence and the restoration of customary Indian craftsmanship, handloom winding around, and other homegrown enterprises. This development was a reaction to the monetary double-dealing and deindustrialization that happened under English provincial rule, as the Indian economy was intensely situated towards serving English interests.

The Swadeshi development, with its accentuation on monetary independence and confidence, was a vital second in India's industrialization process. It electrifies support for Indian-made items as well as encouraged a feeling of business venture and development. Native enterprises started to recover conspicuousness, and customary abilities and craftsmanship were revived.

The mid twentieth century saw the ascent of Mahatma Gandhi as a conspicuous head of the Indian freedom development. Gandhi's vision of monetary independence, in light of the standards of straightforward living and confidence, significantly impacted the direction of India's industrialization. He supported for the advancement of limited scope and house ventures to advance independence at the grassroots level.

Gandhi's way of thinking of "Sarvodaya," or the government assistance of all, enveloped financial and social aspects. His advancement of Khadi, a hand-turned and hand-woven texture, represented independence and the strengthening of country networks. The Khadi development meant to work on the monetary states of the country poor by empowering turning and winding around, furnishing them with a type of revenue.

The Indian Public Congress, under the authority of Jawaharlal Nehru, assumed a focal part in forming the financial strategies of post-freedom India. Nehru's vision of a blended economy, joining components of both communism and free enterprise, looked to accomplish a harmony among public and confidential areas.

This approach was revered in the Modern Arrangement Goal of 1948, which established the groundwork for India's industrialization in the post-autonomy time.

One of the essential goals of post-autonomy modern approaches was to diminish monetary incongruities and inspire the oppressed areas of society. The Five-Year Plans, started in 1951, pointed toward accomplishing self-supported monetary development and evenhanded conveyance of riches. These plans stressed industrialization for of advancing monetary turn of events and lessening destitution.

The emphasis on weighty businesses, foundation improvement, and logical examination was a characterizing component of post-freedom industrialization endeavors. The foundation of key establishments, like the Indian Establishments of Innovation (IITs) and the Indian Space Exploration Association (ISRO), showed a promise to mechanical headway and development. These establishments assumed significant parts in molding India's modern and mechanical scene.

One of the main modern accomplishments during this period was the improvement of the public area. The public authority assumed a focal part in key ventures like steel, coal, and large equipment. The foundation of public area endeavors, for example, Steel Authority of India Restricted (SAIL) and Bharat Weighty Electricals Restricted (BHEL), expected to make a powerful modern base and guarantee command over essential areas of the economy.

The Green Unrest, started during the 1960s, was one more achievement in India's industrialization process. It zeroed in on farming efficiency and expected to change India from a food-lacking country to an independent one. The presentation of high-yielding harvest assortments, further developed water system methods, and admittance to current rural hardware essentially helped horticultural creation.

The impact of the autonomy development on industrialization was not restricted to monetary approaches; it likewise had social and social ramifications. The accentuation on confidence, decentralization, and strengthening of provincial networks changed the elements of India's modern scene. It prompted the advancement of limited scope and cabin enterprises, handloom winding around, and painstaking work.

In the post-freedom period, the recovery of handlooms and painstaking work turned into an image of India's social and monetary resurgence. Associations like the Khadi and Town Enterprises Commission (KVIC) were laid out to advance and support country businesses. These endeavors safeguarded customary abilities and craftsmanship as well as produced work valuable open doors in country regions.

The job of the freedom development in molding India's modern scene stretched out to the advancement of native innovations and logical exploration.

Visionaries like Vikram Sarabhai, the dad of the Indian space program, attempted to saddle the capability of room innovation for public turn of events. The foundation of ISRO and its ensuing accomplishments in space investigation exhibited India's mechanical ability.

The impact of the autonomy development on industrialization likewise stretched out to the advancement of schooling and exploration. The establishing of IITs and other scholarly organizations intended to sustain a culture of development and innovative greatness. These establishments became centers for innovative work, delivering a gifted labor force that added to different modern areas.

The post-autonomy period saw India's modern scene broaden and grow. Businesses like drugs, data innovation, and broadcast communications saw critical development. The drug business, for example, turned into a worldwide player, delivering excellent nonexclusive meds and immunizations. The IT area, with its emphasis on programming improvement and administrations, made a specialty in the worldwide market.

The job of key trailblazers and visionaries in the post-autonomy period kept on being instrumental in molding India's industrialization. The commitments of people like Dhirubhai Ambani, the pioneer behind Dependence Ventures, denoted the rise of private area business. Ambani's vision and business sharpness prompted the development of Dependence into different enterprises, including petrochemicals, materials, and media communications.

Moreover, India's progression approaches during the 1990s, driven by pioneers like Dr. Manmohan Singh, intended to open up the economy to worldwide exchange and speculation. These arrangements empowered unfamiliar direct venture, advanced privatization, and considered more prominent cooperation of the confidential area in different enterprises. The progression period denoted a huge change in India's modern scene, cultivating monetary development, development, and seriousness.

The impact of the freedom development on industrialization was not restricted to financial strategies and modern areas. It likewise included social and natural aspects. Endeavors to lessen destitution, advance civil rights, and further develop expectations for everyday comforts were fundamental to the vision of a free India.

The development of ventures assumed a pivotal part in producing work potential open doors and working on expectations for everyday comforts. The financial improvement that followed freedom added to a critical decrease in neediness rates and a development of the working class. Nonetheless, difficulties of pay imbalance and incongruities among metropolitan and provincial regions continued.

The natural effect of industrialization turned into a developing worry in the post-freedom time. The industrialization cycle, especially in weighty ventures and asset escalated areas, brought up issues about maintainable turn of events and ecological preservation.

Approaches and drives were acquainted with address natural difficulties and advance supportable practices in enterprises.

The impact of the freedom development on industrialization stretched out to the improvement of a different and pluralistic culture. India's obligation to vote based standards, secularism, and social variety was fundamental to its way of life as a country. These standards molded the socio-social texture and upsides of Indian culture, affecting modern practices, corporate administration, and social obligation.

The job of trailblazers and visionaries in post-autonomy India was not restricted to the business world; it stretched out to different areas, including science, innovation, social change, and administration. Figures like A.P.J. Abdul Kalam, known as the "Rocket Man of India," made critical commitments to India's guard and space programs. Kalam's visionary administration and obligation to mechanical progression were vital in molding the country's logical and innovative abilities.

The effect of the freedom development on industrialization was additionally reflected in the advancement of social business venture and corporate social obligation (CSR). Visionaries like Ratan Goodbye, through drives like the Goodbye Trusts, accentuated the important.

Chapter 2

"Forging the Foundations: Steel and Metallurgy"

The historical backdrop of human civilization is interlaced with the turn of events and dominance of metallurgy. The capacity to remove, control, and shape metals denoted a huge move toward our advancement as an animal varieties. Among every one of the metals, steel stands apart as perhaps of the most extraordinary and flexible material throughout the entire existence of industry. The manufacturing of steel and the development of metallurgy play had a vital impact in significantly shaping social orders, economies, and mechanical headways.

Metallurgy, the science and craft of separating and handling metals from minerals, has a long and celebrated history. It is accepted to have started in the late Stone Age when early people found the extraordinary force of intensity on specific rocks. The most common way of purifying, which includes warming minerals to extricate metals, established the groundwork for metallurgical headways. Early civilizations like the Sumerians and Egyptians started to use copper and bronze, which are composites of copper, tin, and different components, for different instruments and antiques.

The Iron Age, which followed the Bronze Age, denoted a critical jump in metallurgical capacities. Iron, plentiful in nature, offered a few benefits over bronze, including more noteworthy strength and solidness. The Hittites in Anatolia (cutting edge Turkey) are attributed with being among quick to foster iron purifying procedures around 1200 BCE. The broad reception of iron devices and weaponry continuously supplanted bronze, introducing another time of mechanical advancement.

Steel, a combination basically made out of iron and carbon, assumed a basic part in the headway of metallurgy. The change of iron into steel was a critical metallurgical forward leap, as it improved the metal's properties, making it more grounded and more tough. Early steel-production procedures depended on the dissemination of carbon into iron, regularly through warming and extinguishing processes. These techniques laid the foundation for the advancement of great steel.

One of the most famous authentic focuses of steel creation was antiquated India. The district was known for its high level metallurgical practices, especially the creation of great cauldron steel. Indian craftsmans excelled at making Wootz steel, which was profoundly valued for its excellent hardness and sharpness. Wootz steel was popular all around the world, with swords and edges produced using it becoming incredible for their prevalent quality.

The most common way of making Wootz steel included the continued warming, liquefying, and manufacturing of iron and carbon-rich materials in pots. This work serious technique created ingots of outstandingly unadulterated steel, which were then used to make fine edges. The Damascus steel, utilized in the renowned blades of the Center East, was one more type of pot steel, known for its particular examples and uncommon ability to cut.

Steel creation additionally flourished in antiquated China, where methods for making steel date back to essentially the second century BCE. Chinese metallurgists used shoot heaters to deliver cast iron, a forerunner to steel. The utilization of solid metal denoted a critical headway in iron and steel innovation. While it was not generally so pliable as steel, cast iron was great for the development of different instruments and carries out.

The spread of steel-production methods, alongside the trading of information through shipping lanes like the Silk Street, added to the worldwide dispersion of metallurgical headways. These improvements significantly affected different social orders and assumed a vital part in the ascent and fall of developments.

The Medieval times in Europe saw the resurgence of iron and steel creation, with mechanical progressions in metalworking. The foundation of water-fueled plants and the use of water wheels for mechanical work worked on the productivity of metalworking processes. The impact heater, a vital improvement during this period, empowered the huge scope creation of solid metal and pig iron, establishing the groundwork for the iron and steel ventures.

Archaic Europe likewise saw the development of organizations, relationship of gifted skilled workers and craftsmans. These societies assumed a focal part in the guideline and dispersal of metallurgical information. Individuals from these societies were liable for creating a large number of metal items, including instruments, weapons, and protection. The society framework kept up with quality guidelines as well as encouraged the exchange of metallurgical mastery starting with one age then onto the next.

The Renaissance time frame achieved a flood in logical request and mechanical development. Developments in hardware, for example, the improvement of the water-fueled hammer and the utilization of coal for warming, denoted a huge step in the right direction in the steel business. These progressions made ready for more proficient and dependable steel creation techniques, powering the development of assembling and exchange.

The early current time frame in Europe saw the foundation of the principal modern scale ironworks and steel plants. Abraham Darby, an English ironmaster, is famous for his spearheading work in the utilization of coke, a subordinate of coal, in iron refining. This development, known as the "coke purifying cycle," was a critical jump in iron and steel creation. It prompted the improvement of the world's most memorable iron extension, known as the Iron Scaffold, in 1779.

One more vital figure throughout the entire existence of metallurgy was Henry Bessemer, an English creator. During the nineteenth hundred years, Bessemer fostered the Bessemer interaction, a progressive strategy for changing over pig iron into steel. The cycle included blowing air through liquid iron to eliminate contaminations and control carbon content, bringing about the creation of great steel. The Bessemer cycle, later refined by others, fundamentally diminished the expense of steel creation and sped up industrialization.

All the while, developments in the utilization of steam power and mechanical designing extraordinarily affected the steel business. The advancement of steam motors and the use of steam power in plants and processing plants prompted more noteworthy productivity and expanded creation limit. Steam-controlled moving factories, for instance, considered the large scale manufacturing of steel items, including rails, shafts, and plates, which were pivotal for the extension of rail routes and framework.

The coming of the railroad was a stupendous occasion throughout the entire existence of the steel business. The development of rail lines required immense amounts of steel, including rails, trains, and moving stock. The extension of rail routes worked with the development of individuals, merchandise, and assets, prompting financial development and industrialization. Steel turned into a fundamental material for building the quickly extending organization of rail routes around the world.

The US assumed a focal part in the worldwide steel industry during the late nineteenth and mid twentieth hundreds of years. The overflow of iron metal and coal, alongside mechanical developments, permitted the U.S. to arise as a significant steel-delivering country. Figures like Andrew Carnegie, the pioneer behind U.S. Steel, assumed a urgent part in this time of modern development.

Carnegie's methodology of vertical joining, which included controlling all parts of the steel creation process, from mining to assembling to dissemination, altogether upgraded the productivity and seriousness of the steel business.

U.S. Steel, established in 1901, turned into the world's initial billion-dollar partnership and exemplified the scale and extent of American industrialization.

The impact of steel on the advancement of the US was colossal. Steel was fundamental for building high rises, extensions, and processing plants. The improvement of the electric curve heater, a strategy for delivering steel through electrical warming, further extended steel creation limit and differentiated the sorts of steel items that could be produced.

The Second Great War and The Second Great War prompted critical headways in steel creation. The requests of fighting required monstrous amounts of steel for weaponry, boats, tanks, and foundation. The advancement of new steel combinations and procedures, like the fundamental oxygen heater (BOF), worked on the quality and strength of steel, making it more reasonable for military and modern applications.

The post-war time frame saw the quick development of the steel business on a worldwide scale. Steel turned into an image of monetary thriving and mechanical headway. It assumed a crucial part in the reproduction of war-torn countries, the extension of foundation, and the development of shopper merchandise enterprises.

The US, Japan, and Western Europe arose as the main steel-creating districts, all in all known as the "Huge Three" in the worldwide steel industry. The improvement of coordinated steel factories, which consolidated all phases of steel creation in a solitary office, turned into a sign of this period. These factories were outfitted with cutting edge innovation and utilized enormous labor forces to satisfy the developing need for steel.

The last part of the twentieth century brought the two open doors and difficulties for the steel business. The development of the worldwide economy and the development of framework in developing business sectors drove the interest for steel. In any case, the business likewise confronted ecological worries, changes in product costs, and expanded contest.

The improvement of cutting edge innovations, for example, consistent projecting and slight chunk projecting, worked on the proficiency and nature of steel creation. These advancements diminished waste and energy utilization while expanding the efficiency of steel plants. Furthermore, the reusing of steel scrap, known as optional steel creation, turned into a huge piece of the business, moderating assets and decreasing ecological effects.

2.1 The rise of the steel industry in India

The steel business plays had an imperative impact in the industrialization and monetary improvement of India. From its humble starting points in the late nineteenth 100 years to turning into the second-biggest steel maker on the planet, India's steel process is a surprising story of diligence, development, and vital preparation. This story digs into the advancement and development of the steel business in India, analyzing the variables and key achievements that have impelled it to its ongoing unmistakable quality.

The starting points of the steel business in India can be followed back to the pioneer time frame when the English laid out the main current steel plant in the country. The Goodbye Iron and Steel Organization, presently known as Goodbye Steel, was established in 1907 by Jamsetji Goodbye. This undeniable a crucial second in India's industrialization process. Goodbye's vision was not only to deliver steel yet to add to the country's independence and modern development. The foundation of

Goodbye Steel in Jamshedpur, Jharkhand, denoted the start of India's cutting edge steel industry.

One of the essential difficulties looked by Goodbye Steel during its initial years was the acquirement of unrefined components, especially iron metal and coal. Goodbye's creative arrangement was to set up his own iron mineral and coal mineshafts in the close by locales. This incorporated methodology permitted Goodbye Steel to get a reliable stockpile of unrefined components and control the whole presentation process, from mining to steel fabricating. Goodbye's vision for vertical coordination and confidence turned into a core value for the Indian steel industry.

Goodbye Steel took on the most trend setting innovations of the time, including the Bessemer interaction and the open-hearth heater, for steel creation. These advances worked with the creation of excellent steel, which was fundamental for framework improvement and modern development. Goodbye's accentuation on innovative work prompted persistent upgrades in assembling processes, item quality, and cost-proficiency.

The fruitful foundation of Goodbye Steel urged different industrialists to put resources into the steel area. The Birla Gathering, established by Ghanshyam Das Birla, entered the steel business with the foundation of the Birla Jute Assembling Organization in 1919, which later expanded into the creation of iron and steel. This extension denoted the start of the Aditya Birla Gathering's excursion in the steel area.

In the pre-autonomy time, the Indian steel industry was described by the presence of a few confidential area steel organizations, each with its own local concentration. These organizations assumed a significant part in satisfying the developing need for steel in different areas, including rail routes, development, and guard.

The difficulties presented by The Second Great War carried further thoughtfulness regarding the requirement for steel creation in India. The extension of protection related exercises and the development of war foundation required an expansion in homegrown steel creation. This period featured the essential significance of a strong steel industry for public safety and improvement.

Post-freedom, the Indian government perceived the meaning of steel in the country's industrialization and advancement. A progression of strategy drives and modern plans were set up to advance the development of the steel area. The Initial Five-Year Plan, sent off in 1951, underlined the development of steel creation limit and the foundation of coordinated steel plants.

The public authority's part in the steel business turned out to be more articulated, with an emphasis on accomplishing independence in steel creation.

The foundation of public area steel organizations turned into a foundation of India's steel strategy. In 1953, the public authority laid out the Hindustan Steel Restricted (HSL) fully intent on setting up steel plants in different pieces of the country. The establishment stone for the Bhilai Steel Plant in Chhattisgarh, the Rourkela Steel Plant in Odisha, and the Durgapur Steel Plant in West Bengal was laid during this period. These coordinated steel plants denoted a huge jump in India's steel creation limit.

The Bhilai Steel Plant, laid out as a team with the Soviet Association, turned into an image of Indo-Soviet participation and mechanical exchange. The plant was furnished with the most recent advances, including the open-hearth heater, and assumed an essential part in the creation of steel for development and foundation improvement.

Essentially, the Rourkela Steel Plant and the Durgapur Steel Plant became significant supporters of the nation's steel creation. These plants produced business potential open doors as well as upheld territorial financial turn of events. The foundation of these public area steel organizations established the groundwork for the development and extension of India's steel industry.

The Second Five-Year Plan, sent off in 1956, underscored the requirement for modernization and development of existing steel plants. The reception of trend setting innovations, including the electric bend heater, considered expanded steel creation and further developed item quality. The public area's part in the steel business was additionally established with the production of the Steel Authority of India Restricted (SAIL) in 1973. SAIL turned into the lead association liable for supervising and overseeing public area steel plants.

During this period, the Indian government kept on zeroing in on independence in steel creation and attempted the foundation of new steel plants. The Bokaro Steel Plant in Jharkhand and the Visakhapatnam Steel Plant in Andhra Pradesh were laid out as a feature of these endeavors. These plants, outfitted with cutting edge advances, assumed a crucial part in satisfying the nation's developing need for steel.

Quite possibly of the main achievement in India's steel industry was the reception of the Maharatna Board of trustees suggestions in 1977. These proposals meant to rebuild the current steel plants, work on their proficiency, and support rivalry inside the area. This approach encouraged development and mechanical headways, bringing about expanded steel creation.

The reception of the Maharatna Advisory group suggestions prompted the arrangement of Rashtriya Ispat Nigam Restricted (RINL), which works the Visakhapatnam Steel Plant. RINL denoted a takeoff from the customary public area structure and embraced more noteworthy independence in direction and tasks.

The 1990s achieved a change in India's monetary strategies, with a move towards progression and globalization. The steel business was not insusceptible to these changes. The opening up of the Indian economy to unfamiliar speculation and contest essentially affected the steel area. Confidential area organizations, both homegrown and worldwide, entered the market, adding to expanded rivalry and mechanical advancement.

The time of advancement and monetary changes prompted the foundation of new steel plants and the extension of existing ones. Confidential area organizations like Jindal Steel and Power Restricted (JSPL), Essar Steel, and Goodbye Steel, among others, became noticeable players in the business. These organizations embraced trend setting innovations, including the electric curve heater and consistent projecting, to upgrade steel creation and item quality.

The development of the Indian steel industry during this period was likewise filled by expanding request from the development, auto, and foundation areas. The development of urbanization and the development of current foundation, including roadways, scaffolds, and air terminals, drove the requirement for steel items. Moreover, the expanding auto industry made a significant market for top notch steel, particularly for the creation of cars and parts.

The 21st century saw further combination and development in India's steel industry. The obtaining of worldwide steel organizations by Indian combinations, like Goodbye Steel's procurement of Corus Gathering and JSW Steel's securing of Acero Property, meant India's development as a worldwide player in the steel area.

The reception of cutting edge innovations, including the utilization of electric circular segment heaters, persistent projecting, and present day moving factories, added to the expansion in steel creation limit and item variety. The Indian steel industry started to zero in on the creation of significant worth added steel items, including exceptional prepares, tempered steels, and high level high-strength prepares, to take special care of assorted modern requirements.

India's steel industry likewise gained huge headway concerning maintainability and natural obligation. Endeavors were made to decrease energy utilization, limit fossil fuel byproducts, and improve asset use. The improvement of green steel advances, for example, direct decrease utilizing petroleum gas and the utilization of sustainable power sources, meant to make steel creation all the more harmless to the ecosystem.

The Make in India drive, sent off in 2014, further highlighted the significance of the assembling area, including the steel business, in India's financial development. The drive intended to advance homegrown assembling, draw in unfamiliar speculation, and encourage development. It gave force to the Indian steel industry to extend and enhance its capacities.

The Public Steel Strategy of 2017 set an objective of accomplishing 300 million metric lots of steel creation limit by 2030. The approach zeroed in on improving the seriousness of the steel business, advancing innovative work, and tending to ecological worries.

It additionally looked to energize interest in the steel area and guarantee its commitment to the development of partnered enterprises and work age.

The Coronavirus pandemic in 2020 presented phenomenal difficulties to the steel business, remembering disturbances for the store network, a drop popular, and the need to guarantee the security of the labor force. In any case, the Indian steel industry exhibited .

2.2 Profiles of iconic steel plants like Tata Steel and Bhilai Steel Plant

The steel business has been a foundation of industrialization and financial improvement in India. Throughout the long term, a few famous steel plants play had a urgent impact in forming the country's modern scene. Among these, Goodbye Steel and the Bhilai Steel Plant have arisen as images of development, independence, and innovative headway. This story gives a definite profile of these famous steel plants and their critical commitments to India's steel industry.

Goodbye Steel: A Tradition of Greatness

Goodbye Steel, previously known as the Goodbye Iron and Steel Organization (TISCO), is one of the most eminent and noteworthy steel plants in India. Laid out in 1907 by the visionary industrialist Jamsetji Goodbye, Goodbye Steel denoted the start of the advanced steel industry in India. Its excursion from commencement to turning into a worldwide steel monster is a demonstration of development, steadiness, and a pledge to country building.

Establishing and Vision: The foundation of Goodbye Steel was driven by Jamsetji Goodbye's visionary standards of independence and modern advancement. He perceived the essential significance of steel for India's development and improvement. Goodbye's vision was not only to deliver steel yet to establish the groundworks for a confident and industrialized India.

To accomplish this vision, Goodbye Steel was established in Sakchi, a far off town in the territory of Bihar (presently Jharkhand). The area was decided because of its vicinity to rich iron mineral and coal holds, significant unrefined components for steel creation. The plant was decisively positioned close to the conversion of the Subarnarekha and Kharkai streams, guaranteeing a predictable stock of water, one more fundamental prerequisite for steel fabricating.

Vertical Combination: Jamsetji Goodbye had faith in the standards of vertical mix, which included controlling the whole presentation process, from mining to assembling. This approach permitted Goodbye Steel to get a consistent inventory of unrefined components and exercise command over the whole steel creation chain.

Goodbye Steel laid out its own iron mineral and coal mineshafts in the areas encompassing the plant. This approach not just guaranteed a ceaseless inventory of fundamental unrefined components yet in addition prompted the improvement of a confident and independent modern complex. The incorporated model turned into an outline for the eventual fate of the Indian steel industry.

Innovative Headways: Goodbye Steel rushed to embrace the most cutting edge innovations of now is the ideal time, including the Bessemer cycle and the open-hearth heater. These advancements added to the creation of great steel, which was fundamental for framework improvement, modern development, and protection necessities.

Goodbye Steel's obligation to innovative work prompted persistent upgrades in assembling processes, item quality, and cost-proficiency. The organization's accentuation on development and variation to arising advances assumed a urgent part in its prosperity.

Local area and Government assistance: Jamsetji Goodbye was worried about modern advancement as well as with the government assistance of the labor force and the networks around the plant. He presented a few moderate drives, including giving lodging, medical care, and schooling for the workers and their families. Goodbye Steel's model municipality, Jamshedpur, was planned with an emphasis on arranged metropolitan turn of events, green spaces, and exhaustive conveniences for occupants.

Goodbye Steel's obligation to corporate social obligation stretched out to the more extensive local area also. The organization was engaged with local area advancement programs, medical care offices, and instructive foundations. The Goodbye Iron and Steel Organization turned into a model of moral and socially mindful strategic approaches.

Worldwide Impression: Throughout the long term, Goodbye Steel extended its presence past India. The securing of Corus Gathering (previously English Steel) in 2007 denoted a critical achievement in the organization's worldwide excursion. It was quite possibly of the biggest abroad procurement by an Indian organization at that point and situated Goodbye Steel as one of the world's driving steel makers.

Goodbye Steel's worldwide impression extended further with tasks in the Unified Realm, Europe, and Southeast Asia. The organization kept on putting resources into innovation, development, and economical practices to keep up with its situation as a main player in the worldwide steel industry.

Bhilai Steel Plant: An Image of Indo-Soviet Collaboration

The Bhilai Steel Plant, arranged in Bhilai, Chhattisgarh, is one of the most huge and famous steel plants in India. Its foundation during the 1950s denoted a noteworthy part in the country's industrialization and the start of Indo-Soviet collaboration in the field of steel creation. The plant is eminent for its mechanical headways, quality steel creation, and job in country building.

Establishment and Collaboration: The establishment stone for the Bhilai Steel Plant was laid by Dr. Rajendra Prasad, the main Leader of India, on June 30, 1955. The plant was a consequence of coordinated effort between the states of India and the Soviet Association, under the specialized direction of the Soviet designers. The venture was a sign of India's obligation to accomplishing independence in steel creation.

The participation with the Soviet Association permitted Bhilai Steel Plant to get to cutting edge innovations and mastery in steel producing. The plant was outfitted with the most recent advances, including the open-hearth heater, and was intended to deliver excellent steel for development and framework improvement.

Mechanical Development: The Bhilai Steel Plant immediately earned respect for its innovative headways. It turned into the first plant in Quite a while to embrace the Paul Wurth process for coke making, which essentially worked on the effectiveness and nature of coke creation. The plant likewise presented nonstop projecting innovation without precedent for the nation, further upgrading the nature of steel items.

The plant's reception of the Kaldo converter, a high level steelmaking process, expanded steel creation limit and worked on the nature of steel. Bhilai Steel Plant's obligation to mechanical development and modernization assumed a urgent part in the development of the Indian steel industry.

Business and Provincial Turn of events: The foundation of the Bhilai Steel Plant produced critical work potential open doors in the area. It pulled in a different labor force from different pieces of the nation, adding to social variety and social joining. The plant assumed a vital part in the monetary improvement of Bhilai and the encompassing regions.

The plant's municipality, Bhilai, was arranged with an emphasis on giving complete conveniences and administrations to its inhabitants. The foundation of instructive organizations, medical care offices, and sporting spaces advanced the personal satisfaction for the representatives and their families.

Bhilai's Commitment: Bhilai Steel Plant's commitment to the country's modern and infrastructural improvement was significant. The plant provided excellent steel for different areas, including development, railroads, guard, and assembling. Its job in creating rails, underlying steel, and other key materials was necessary to the development of the Indian rail line organization and the development of present day framework.

The Bhilai Steel Plant likewise assumed a critical part in the protection area, providing steel for military gear and vehicles. Its steady creation and quality norms made it a solid wellspring of steel for basic applications.

Green Drives: as of late, the Bhilai Steel Plant has zeroed in on taking on green advancements and supportable practices. Endeavors have been made to diminish energy utilization, limit natural effect, and streamline asset use. The plant has carried out measures to further develop energy effectiveness and diminish fossil fuel byproducts.

The fate of Bhilai Steel Plant is lined up with the standards of ecological obligation and asset protection. The plant's obligation to practical steel creation highlights its part in India's excursion toward a greener and more mindful modern scene.

Commitments to India's Industrialization

Both Goodbye Steel and the Bhilai Steel Plant have made critical commitments to India's industrialization, foundation improvement, and independence in steel creation. Their accounts embody the force of vision, development, and obligation to country building.

Goodbye Steel's accentuation on vertical combination, mechanical progressions, and corporate social obligation set an elevated requirement for the steel business in India. The organization's development and worldwide extension are a demonstration of its initiative in the worldwide steel market.

The Bhilai Steel Plant's job in Indo-Soviet participation, mechanical advancement, and territorial improvement epitomizes the soul of coordinated effort and confidence. The plant's constant spotlight on modernization and supportability lines up with India's contemporary objectives for the steel business.

The traditions of Goodbye Steel and the Bhilai Steel Plant stretch out past steel creation. They mirror the modern and financial change of the locales where they are arranged. The two organizations have added to the improvement of model municipalities, giving schooling, medical services, and sporting offices to their workers and networks.

The Indian steel industry's development from the provincial time frame to the current day is interlaced with the chronicles of these notorious steel plants. Their spearheading endeavors and obligation to greatness lastingly affect India's modern scene.

2.3 The impact of steel production on the Indian economy

The Indian steel industry has for quite some time been perceived as an indispensable mainstay of the country's monetary development and modern turn of events. The creation and utilization of steel have significant ramifications for different areas, going from development and framework to auto and assembling. This story investigates the diverse effect of steel creation on the Indian economy, enveloping its job as a driver of development, business generator, and supporter of framework improvement.

Monetary Development and Industrialization

The Indian steel industry has been a critical driver of monetary development and industrialization. Steel is considered an essential material for current modern social orders, and its creation mirrors the degree of modern movement in a country. The steel area in India plays had a significant impact in supporting and supporting monetary turn of events. Here are a portion of the essential manners by which the steel business has added to monetary development:

Foundation Improvement: Steel is the foundation of framework advancement. It is a basic part in the development of streets, spans, dams, air terminals, and public structures.

The interest for steel in the development area has been consistently expanding with the extension of metropolitan regions and the requirement for current foundation. As India keeps on putting resources into framework projects, the steel business assumes a central part in giving the vital materials.

Industrialization: Steel is utilized in different assembling businesses, making it an empowering agent of industrialization. The development of the assembling area depends vigorously on the accessibility of steel for hardware, gear, and instruments. From auto assembling to large equipment creation, the steel business upholds modern broadening and development.

Financial Flexibility: The steel business' flexibility and adaptability make it a tough area, fit for enduring monetary variances. During times of monetary development, steel request increments as development and assembling exercises extend. Alternately, during financial slumps, steel stays vital for revamping and renewing ventures and foundation.

Business Age: The steel business is a huge wellspring of work, straightforwardly and in a roundabout way. It gives occupations in different areas, including producing, mining, innovative work, and deals and advertising. The steel business' capacity to create work adds to destitution decrease and social prosperity, particularly in districts where steel plants are found.

Work Age and Social Prosperity

The steel business is a significant supporter of work age in India. Its activities set out work open doors across the worth chain, from mining and unrefined substance extraction to steel creation, handling, and promoting. The effect of the steel business on work and social prosperity can be analyzed through the accompanying viewpoints:

Direct Business: Steel plants, particularly huge incorporated steel offices, utilize a critical labor force. Laborers are taken part in different jobs, including plant activities, support, quality control, and organization. The business offers business valuable open doors to a different scope of experts, gifted specialists, and workers.

Circuitous Business: Past the immediate labor force, the steel business animates backhanded work in areas like transportation, strategies, administrations, and development. The inventory network of the steel business includes an immense organization of providers, merchants, and specialist co-ops, all of which produce unexpected open positions.

Monetary Improvement in Steel Groups: Steel bunches, regions with a centralization of steel plants and subordinate enterprises, experience financial development and social turn of events. These bunches draw in labor from encompassing areas, prompting populace movement and confined monetary action. This, thusly, cultivates business and interest in help administrations.

Ability Advancement: The steel business' interest for talented and semi-gifted work has prodded interests in professional preparation and expertise improvement programs.

This has added to the upgrade of human resources, permitting laborers to procure particular abilities and work on their employability.

Social Prosperity: Business potential open doors given by the steel business emphatically affect social prosperity. Professional stability, pay security, and admittance to medical care and schooling administrations add to a superior personal satisfaction for steel industry workers and their families.

Framework Improvement and Urbanization

Steel is a fundamental material for foundation improvement, and the extension of the steel business has been firmly lined up with urbanization in India. The effect of steel creation on framework advancement and urbanization can be seen through a few key aspects:

Development and Lodging: Steel is a key part in the development of private and business structures. The expanded accessibility of steel has considered imaginative engineering plans, underlying solidness, and further developed wellbeing in development. It has additionally upheld the advancement of metropolitan focuses by empowering the development of elevated structures.

Transportation: The transportation area depends on steel for the development of vehicles, rail lines, scaffolds, and streets. The extension of the steel business has worked with the development of transportation foundation, including the development of roadways and the extension of the rail line organization. These advancements have associated metropolitan and rustic regions, driving financial movement and exchange.

Energy Foundation: Steel is utilized in the development of energy framework, for example, power plants, transmission pinnacles, and pipelines. The extension of the steel business has added to the advancement of energy age and appropriation offices, guaranteeing admittance to power for metropolitan and provincial regions the same.

Water Supply and Disinfection: Steel assumes a vital part in the development of water supply and sterilization foundation, including water treatment plants and conveyance pipelines. This has prompted superior admittance to clean drinking water and sterilization offices in metropolitan and peri-metropolitan regions.

Media communications: The development of the media communications area has been firmly connected to the steel business. The development of telecom towers and the establishment of fiber-optic links are dependent on steel. This has worked with the extension of network, further developed admittance to data, and upheld digitalization endeavors in metropolitan and rustic districts.

Exchange and Product Income

The Indian steel industry has been a huge supporter of the nation's exchange and commodity profit. Steel items, both crude and handled, are sent out to global business sectors, creating unfamiliar trade and adding to the nation's exchange balance. The effect of the steel business on exchange and product income can be evaluated through the accompanying perspectives:

Trade Income: The steel business adds to India's commodity profit by offering different steel items to different nations. These items incorporate level steel, long steel, lines, tubes, and concentrated steel items. Sending out steel items upgrades the country's unfamiliar trade saves and exchange execution.

Worldwide Presence: Indian steel organizations have extended their presence in global business sectors. Acquisitions and interests in steel organizations abroad have situated Indian steel makers as worldwide players. The securing of abroad steel plants, like Corus Gathering (previously English Steel) by Goodbye Steel, has extended India's impression in the worldwide steel market.

Unfamiliar Trade Saves: The commodity of steel items brings about the inflow of unfamiliar cash into the Indian economy. This unfamiliar trade can be utilized to fund imports, administration outer obligation, and support the country's unfamiliar trade saves, adding to financial security.

Upper hand: The Indian steel industry enjoys showed its serious benefit by offering quality steel items at cutthroat costs in the worldwide market. This cutthroat estimating has permitted Indian steel makers to get requests and clients in different regions of the planet.

Import Replacement: The homegrown creation of steel has added to diminishing India's reliance on steel imports. By fulfilling homegrown need through neighborhood creation, the nation saves unfamiliar trade that would somehow or another be spent on steel imports.

Natural Supportability and Obligation

The effect of steel creation on the Indian economy stretches out to ecological manageability and corporate obligation. The steel business, as other weighty enterprises, has been under a magnifying glass for its ecological impression. Nonetheless, it has likewise shown its obligation to supportable practices and lessening its natural effect in more ways than one:

Energy Proficiency: The Indian steel industry has embraced endeavors to further develop energy productivity in steel creation. Cutting edge innovations, including electric bend heaters and waste intensity recuperation frameworks, have been embraced to lessen energy utilization and emanations.

Asset Usage: Steel makers have investigated ways of enhancing asset use and limit squander. The reusing of steel scrap, known as optional steel creation, is an essential piece of the business' maintainability endeavors.

It rations assets, diminishes waste, and brings down the carbon impression of steel creation.

Ecological Consistence: The business is dependent upon natural guidelines and norms. Consistence with these guidelines is essential to guarantee dependable ecological practices. Many steel organizations put resources into contamination control hardware and innovations to limit outflows and safeguard the climate.

Chapter 3

"Powering the Nation: Energy and Infrastructure"

Energy and framework are the twin motors that drive a country's financial development and improvement. On account of India, a country with a quickly extending populace and aggressive improvement objectives, the job of energy and foundation turns out to be significantly more basic. This story digs into the entwined development of energy and framework in India, investigating their effect on monetary advancement, social prosperity, and the nation's mission for independence.

Energy and Framework: The Underpinnings of Improvement

Energy and framework are the foundations of monetary turn of events. They are inseparably connected, with energy being the backbone that drives the framework vital for current living. With regards to India, a nation portrayed by its segment profit and an expanding working class, the interest for energy and the requirement for powerful framework have never been more articulated.

The connection among energy and framework is advantageous. Framework advancement requires energy, and energy foundation requires deep rooted actual framework for its age, transmission, and dispersion. How about we dig into the entwined excursion of energy and foundation in India, analyzing how they have been significant in forming the country's turn of events.

The Advancing Energy Scene

India's energy process has navigated a different scene, incorporating customary energy sources, petroleum derivatives, environmentally friendly power, and atomic power. The country's energy needs have filled dramatically in light of industrialization, urbanization, and the rising goals of its populace.

Conventional Energy Sources: All things considered, India has depended on customary energy sources like biomass, wood, and creature fertilizer for cooking and warming. These sources, while available and moderately minimal expense, have natural and wellbeing suggestions because of indoor air contamination and deforestation.

Non-renewable energy sources and the Modern Unrest: The modern upheaval in India was fundamentally filled by the approach of petroleum derivatives, especially coal. Coal turned into the foundation of energy age, driving the development of ventures, rail lines, and metropolitan focuses. The English frontier rulers laid out coal mineshafts to drive steam motors and work with the transportation of unrefined components and products.

Post-autonomy, the significance of coal kept on developing. India's coal saves became pivotal for supporting energy needs and modern development. Coal-terminated power plants assumed a significant part in giving power to homes, production lines, and organizations.

Oil and Gas*: The revelation of oil and gas saves in India's western and northeastern areas changed the energy scene. The extraction of petrol assets and the foundation of treatment facilities extended the accessibility of oil based commodities, including gas, diesel, and flying fills. The development of the car business and the flight area was impelled by the availability of these fills.

The time of financial progression during the 1990s saw expanded unfamiliar interest in the oil and gas area. Investigation and creation exercises extended, further differentiating the energy blend. Gaseous petrol, specifically, acquired conspicuousness as a cleaner and more productive fuel source.

Atomic Power*: India's introduction to atomic power age started during the 1960s with the foundation of the Nuclear Energy Commission. The country's serene atomic blasts in 1974 denoted a huge achievement in its atomic excursion, which has since been centered around both energy age and examination.

Thermal power enjoys the benefit of being a low-carbon and high-limit wellspring of force. India has a few thermal energy stations, incorporating those with native Compressed Weighty Water Reactors (PHWRs) and joint efforts with nations like Russia and France.

Sustainable Energy*: The developing accentuation on environmentally friendly power sources, especially sun oriented and wind power, has turned into a characterizing component of India's energy scene. The public authority sent off the Jawaharlal Nehru Public Sun oriented Mission in 2010 determined to accomplish 20 GW of sun based power by 2022.

Environmentally friendly power projects have picked up speed with an emphasis on energy productivity, decreased fossil fuel byproducts, and maintainability. India's obligation to environmentally friendly power lines up with its worldwide environmental change liabilities and the quest for a cleaner and greener energy future.

Power Age and Access*: The extension of power age limit has been fundamental in gathering the energy needs of India's developing populace. The improvement of nuclear energy stations, hydropower projects, atomic reactors, and sustainable power establishments has fundamentally expanded power creation.

Further developing admittance to power for rustic and distant regions has been really important. Drives like the Deen Dayal Upadhyaya Gram Jyoti Yojana (DDUGJY) have intended to jolt towns and give last-mile network. The Saubhagya conspire, sent off in 2017, has tried to give power associations with all families, further upgrading energy access.

The Force of Framework

Framework is the actual spine that upholds the conveyance of energy and various other fundamental administrations. Streets, spans, rail routes, air terminals, ports, and metropolitan offices are fundamental to a nation's turn of events. The development of India's foundation scene has been entwined with its energy prerequisites as well as the other way around.

Transport Foundation: The improvement of India's transportation framework has been a critical driver of monetary development. Streets, rail lines, air terminals, and ports work with the development of products, individuals, and administrations. As the interest for energy has developed, the transportation area has depended on solid and productive framework to help its extension.

India's railroad organization, one of the biggest on the planet, is intensely subject to energy, especially diesel for trains and power for zapped courses. The development of interstates and turnpikes has upgraded street network, diminishing travel times and transportation costs. Air terminals, both homegrown and worldwide, have been created to take special care of the developing flight area.

Metropolitan Foundation: India's metropolitan places have encountered quick populace development and urbanization. The improvement of metropolitan framework is fundamental to oblige this segment shift. Solid power supply, water assets, sterilization, and public transportation are fundamental parts of metropolitan foundation.

Metropolitan urban areas like Delhi, Mumbai, and Bangalore have put resources into present day metropolitan transportation frameworks, including metro railroads and transport quick travel frameworks. Water supply and sewage treatment offices are vital for metropolitan cleanliness and prosperity.

Rustic and Farming Framework: The country and rural areas are essential to India's economy. Framework advancement there is critical for working on rural efficiency and livelihoods. The development of country streets, water system frameworks, and cold storage spaces has upheld rural development.

Provincial zap programs have given power to horticultural exercises and homegrown use. The Pradhan Mantri Gram Sadak Yojana (PMGSY) has intended to associate country regions with every single climate street, working with the transportation of agrarian produce.

Energy Framework: The foundation of energy framework incorporates power age offices, transmission and circulation organizations, and energy stockpiling frameworks. Power age limit, substations, and matrix framework are fundamental for conveying power to homes and businesses.

As the interest for sustainable power sources has developed, sun oriented and wind power establishments have multiplied the nation over. These establishments require specific energy foundation, like sunlight powered chargers, wind turbines, and matrix mix advances.

Ports and Sea Framework: India's shoreline along the Middle Eastern Ocean and the Cove of Bengal has worked with sea exchange. The improvement of ports and sea framework plays had a huge impact in supporting global exchange and monetary development.

Significant ports like Mumbai, Chennai, and Kolkata, as well as more current ports like Mundra and Ennore, have extended to deal with bigger freight volumes and oblige present day vessels. This framework has supported India's sea availability with nations in the Indian Sea area.

Data Innovation Foundation: The development of India's data innovation (IT) and programming administrations area has been upheld by vigorous IT framework. Server farms, rapid web availability, and media transmission networks are fundamental for the IT business' activities.

India's IT area has contributed fundamentally to financial development by giving programming improvement and IT administrations to clients all over the planet. The country's innovative capacities have made it a worldwide center point for Itself and programming arrangements.

Energy and Framework: Shared Support

Energy for Framework: The improvement of foundation, whether it's transportation, metropolitan offices, or modern buildings, requires a steady and open energy supply. Energy sources like power, oil, and gas are fundamental for the development and activity of foundation.

Framework for Energy Age: Energy foundation, for example, power plants and transmission lines, requires its own foundation. Power plants require land, cooling water sources, and admittance to fuel supplies. Transmission and dissemination networks need an organization of substations and transmission towers.

Efficient power Energy and Manageable Infrastructure*: The shift towards green and maintainable energy sources is firmly connected to foundation improvement.

3.1 The development of the power sector

The power area is the help of a country's financial development and improvement. In India, a country with a quickly developing populace and aggressive industrialization objectives, the development of the power area has been a groundbreaking excursion. This story investigates the verifiable improvement of the power area in India, looking at its effect on the country's advancement, charge endeavors, difficulties, and valuable open doors.

Early Starting points: The Coming of Power

The tale of India's power area starts with the presentation of power during the late nineteenth and mid twentieth hundreds of years. The frontier period saw the foundation of force age offices in key urban communities to serve the necessities of English organization, rail routes, and industry. Here are a portion of the significant improvements during this period:

Calcutta and Bombay*: The urban communities of Calcutta (presently Kolkata) and Bombay (presently Mumbai) were among the first in Quite a while to encounter electric lighting. The Calcutta Electric Stock Partnership (CESC) was established in 1897, trailed by the Bombay Electric Stock and Tramways Organization in 1905. These organizations denoted the initiation of metropolitan jolt.

Hydroelectric Power*: The early power age basically depended on hydroelectric power plants. The Kundala Hydroelectric Power Plant in Kerala, authorized in 1940, was perhaps the earliest in Indium. Hydroelectricity, created from streaming water, held guarantee for spotless and environmentally friendly power.

Limited scope Power Generation*: notwithstanding huge hydroelectric activities, limited scope power age was likewise investigated. Towns and modern focuses fired setting up their own power stations, frequently energized by coal or oil. These confined power age offices tended to nearby requirements.

Post-Autonomy Development: Power for the Country

India's freedom in 1947 denoted a defining moment in the improvement of the power area. The public authority perceived the requirement for ability to drive the country's industrialization, modernization, and monetary development. A few key improvements denoted this time:

The Bhakra-Nangal Project*: The Bhakra-Nangal Venture, situated in the territory of Punjab, was one of the main water asset advancement projects in post-autonomy India. Finished during the 1960s, it incorporated the development of the Bhakra Dam and a few different repositories, channels, and forces to be reckoned with. The venture assumed an imperative part in giving water to water system and producing hydroelectric power.

Nationalization of Electricity*: The Power (Supply) Demonstration of 1948 prepared for the nationalization of power supply organizations. State Power Sheets (SEBs) were laid out to assume control over the possession, activity, and the board of force age, transmission, and conveyance.

Quick Expansion*: The period from the 1950s to the 1970s saw a critical development of force age limit. A few nuclear energy stations, involving coal and oil as fuel, were gotten up in a position satisfy the rising need for power. These plants assumed a critical part in energizing the nation and fueling its enterprises.

Hydroelectric Projects*: India's huge hydroelectric potential was tapped through the development of a few tasks. The Bakra Beas The executives Board (BBMB) developed dams and forces to be reckoned with on the Beas Waterway, further saddling hydroelectricity. Projects like the Bhakra-Nangal and Hirakud Dam have been instrumental in both power age and water system.

Public Nuclear energy Partnership (NTPC)*: The NTPC was laid out in 1975 as a public area organization with the command to speed up power age. It assumed an essential part in the development of coal-based nuclear energy stations, and it has since advanced into one of the biggest power makers in India.

Jolting India: Growing Admittance to Power

Jolting the tremendous and various country of India was a stupendous errand. Giving admittance to power to all residents, especially those in provincial and far off regions, was a continuous mission. A few key drives added to growing admittance to power:

Country Electrification*: The Rajiv Gandhi Grameen Vidyutikaran Yojana (RGGVY), sent off in 2005, planned to zap towns and villas. The program stretched out power associations with rustic regions, improving the personal satisfaction and supporting monetary exercises.

Public Charge Mission*: The Pradhan Mantri Sahaj Bijli Har Ghar Yojana, or Saubhagya, sent off in 2017, looked to give power associations with all families, remembering those for metropolitan and far off regions. Saubhagya meant to kill the last-mile network hole and carry power to each home.

Off-Framework and Decentralized Power*: Off-matrix and decentralized power arrangements, including sunlight based scaled down lattices and family planetary groups, play had a huge impact in giving power to far off regions where network is testing. These frameworks have further developed energy access and enabled networks.

Changes in Power Distribution*: The rebuilding of force appropriation organizations (DISCOMs) has been a continuous cycle. Changes planned to work on the monetary soundness of DISCOMs, lessen transmission and appropriation misfortunes, and upgrade the nature of administration.

The Changing Energy Blend: A Progress to Clean Energy

As India wrestled with the rising interest for power and worries about ecological maintainability, the power area started to encounter a change in its energy blend. This shift zeroed in on consolidating cleaner and more practical energy sources:

Atomic Power*: India's excursion in atomic power age started with the foundation of the Nuclear Energy Commission in 1948. Thermal power is a low-carbon and high-limit wellspring of force. India has a few thermal energy stations, incorporating those with native Compressed Weighty Water Reactors (PHWRs) and coordinated efforts with nations like Russia and France.

Inexhaustible Energy*: The emphasis on environmentally friendly power sources, especially sunlight based and wind power, has turned into a characterizing element of India's energy scene. The Jawaharlal Nehru Public Sunlight based Mission, sent off in 2010, meant to accomplish 20 GW of sun oriented power by 2022. Renewables have acquired conspicuousness for their energy productivity, diminished fossil fuel byproducts, and supportability.

Wind Power*: India's breeze power limit has seen critical development, making it one of the top breeze power makers on the planet. Wind ranches, situated in states with positive breeze conditions, have tackled breeze energy for power age.

Sunlight based Power*: Sun oriented power has encountered wonderful development, driven by declining sunlight based charger costs and great sunlight based radiation conditions. Sun based parks and housetop sun oriented establishments have become normal, adding to the broadening of the energy blend.

Energy Productivity and Conservation*: Energy effectiveness drives have acquired conspicuousness. The Perform, Accomplish, and Exchange (PAT) plot, sent off by the Department of Energy Proficiency (Honey bee), meant to further develop the energy execution of energy-escalated businesses and decrease energy utilization.

Difficulties and Potential open doors The improvement of the power area in India has been set apart by accomplishments and difficulties. As the country tries to fulfill its developing energy need while sticking to maintainability objectives, it faces a bunch of chances and difficulties:

Energy Security*: Guaranteeing a solid and dependable energy supply stays a test, particularly despite fluctuating worldwide oil costs and international vulnerabilities. Energy broadening and key stores offer open doors for upgrading energy security.

Natural Sustainability*: India faces the test of offsetting energy needs with ecological manageability. The shift towards sustainable power and energy effectiveness rehearses presents amazing open doors for lessening fossil fuel byproducts and limiting ecological effect.

Energy Access*: Growing energy admittance to all residents, especially in remote and underserved regions, stays a basic test. Off-matrix and decentralized energy arrangements, alongside last-mile availability drives, offer open doors for accomplishing general jolt.

Framework Investment*: The advancement of foundation, including power age and transmission offices, requires significant venture. Public-private associations, unfamiliar venture, and inventive supporting models give open doors to framework funding.

Innovation Adoption*: Utilizing cutting edge innovations, like shrewd frameworks, energy capacity, and computerized foundation, can improve the effectiveness and dependability of the power area. Savvy meters and network combination advances offer open doors for further developing energy the board.

Electric Mobility*: The development of electric vehicles (EVs) presents both a test and an open door. EVs can diminish ozone depleting substance emanations and air contamination, however their reception requires the advancement of charging framework and approaches that advance clean transportation.

Energy Efficiency*: Underlining energy effectiveness in businesses, structures, and apparatuses offers potential open doors for diminishing energy utilization and functional expenses. Energy-effective advances and practices can upgrade the supportability of the power area.

3.2 Hydroelectric and thermal power projects

Hydroelectric and nuclear energy projects play had a critical impact in molding India's energy scene and working with its monetary turn of events. These tasks address two particular ways to deal with power age, each with its own arrangement of benefits and difficulties. This account investigates the set of experiences and effect of hydroelectric and nuclear energy projects in India, featuring their commitments to the country's energy needs and financial development.

Hydroelectric Power Ventures

Hydroelectric power, produced from the progression of water, has been a necessary piece of India's energy blend since the mid twentieth hundred years. The country's different topography, portrayed by various streams and bumpy landscape, gives bountiful chances to tackling hydroelectric energy.

Early Hydroelectric Endeavors: The appearance of hydroelectric power in India can be followed back to the mid twentieth 100 years, with the dispatching of limited scope hydroelectric plants. These plants were laid out to serve restricted needs, for example, controlling ventures and lighting metropolitan focuses. Remarkable early activities incorporated the Kundala Hydroelectric Power Plant in Kerala, dispatched in 1940.

Bhakra-Nangal Venture: Quite possibly of the most famous hydroelectric undertaking in India is the Bhakra-Nangal Task. Arranged in the territory of Punjab, this task, finished during the 1960s, incorporated the development of the Bhakra Dam, a few repositories, channels, and forces to be reckoned with. The Bhakra-Nangal Undertaking is a demonstration of India's emphasis on multipurpose stream valley improvement, giving water to water system and producing hydroelectric power.

Hydropower Development: The Bhakra-Nangal Undertaking denoted the start of enormous scope hydroelectric power projects in India. The nation saw the advancement of a few hydroelectric undertakings, incorporating the Hirakud Dam in Odisha and the Damodar Valley Enterprise projects in West Bengal and Jharkhand. These tasks bridled the capability of streams and given clean energy to different areas.

Difficulties and Valuable open doors: Hydroelectric power projects enjoy specific benefits, for example, being a low-carbon energy source and offering the capacity to store water for water system. Be that as it may, they additionally face difficulties, including ecological worries, dislodging of networks, and reliance on occasional precipitation. There are valuable chances to address these difficulties through better preparation, natural relief measures, and maintainable advancement rehearses.

Nuclear energy Tasks

Nuclear energy projects are integral to India's energy age and charge endeavors. These tasks principally depend on the ignition of non-renewable energy sources, like coal, petroleum gas, and oil, to create power. Nuclear energy plays had a critical impact in jolting the country and supporting modern development.

Post-Autonomy Development: In the wake of acquiring freedom, India set out on an aggressive program of industrialization and modernization. The development of nuclear energy projects was instrumental in giving power to modern necessities, metropolitan focuses, and families. Coal, as a promptly accessible asset, turned into the foundation of nuclear energy age.

Public Nuclear energy Company (NTPC): The foundation of the Public Nuclear energy Partnership (NTPC) in 1975 denoted a huge improvement in the extension of nuclear energy limit. NTPC, a public area organization, assumed a critical part in expanding the age of coal-based nuclear energy. It has since developed into one of the biggest power makers in India.

Coal-Based Power Plants: Coal-terminated power plants turned into a predominant wellspring of power in India. The country's coal saves are plentiful, and coal-terminated power age was viewed as a fundamental source to fulfill the developing energy need. Plants like the Korba Very Nuclear energy Station in Chhattisgarh and the Mundra Ultra Super Power Plant in Gujarat contributed altogether to control age.

Petroleum gas and Oil*: notwithstanding coal, India investigated the utilization of flammable gas and oil for power age. Gaseous petrol power plants, for example, those in the Krishna-Godavari Bowl, offered cleaner choices to coal. Oil-terminated power plants, albeit more uncommon, additionally added to power age.

Difficulties and Valuable open doors: Nuclear energy projects have been fundamental in giving power to a quickly developing populace and growing businesses. Be that as it may, they face difficulties connected with ecological contamination, fossil fuel byproducts, and asset supportability. Potential open doors exist to address these difficulties through cleaner innovations, energy proficiency measures, and a progress to elective fills.

The Changing Energy Blend

The development of India's power area mirrors a progress in the energy blend as the nation looks to offset its energy needs with ecological manageability and energy security.

Atomic Power: India's excursion in atomic power age started during the 1940s with the foundation of the Nuclear Energy Commission. Thermal power is a low-carbon and high-limit wellspring of force. The country has a few thermal energy stations, incorporating those with native Compressed Weighty Water Reactors (PHWRs) and joint efforts with nations like Russia and France.

Environmentally friendly power: The emphasis on environmentally friendly power sources, especially sun oriented and wind power, has turned into a characterizing element of India's energy scene. The Jawaharlal Nehru Public Sun oriented

Mission, sent off in 2010, meant to accomplish 20 GW of sun based power by 2022. Renewables have acquired noticeable quality for their energy effectiveness, decreased fossil fuel byproducts, and manageability.

Wind Power: India's breeze power limit has seen critical development, making it one of the top breeze power makers on the planet. Wind ranches, situated in states with good wind conditions, have tackled breeze energy for power age.

Sun based Power: Sun oriented power has encountered amazing development, driven by declining sunlight based charger costs and ideal sun powered radiation conditions. Sun powered parks and roof sun based establishments have become normal, adding to the expansion of the energy blend.

Energy Productivity and Preservation: Energy proficiency drives have acquired conspicuousness. The Perform, Accomplish, and Exchange (PAT) plot, sent off by the Agency of Energy Effectiveness (Honey bee), meant to further develop the energy execution of energy-escalated businesses and lessen energy utilization.

The Difficulties and Valuable open doors Ahead

As India keeps on developing its energy scene, it faces a bunch of difficulties and valuable open doors:

Ecological Manageability: Adjusting the developing energy interest with natural maintainability is a key test. The progress to cleaner energy sources, energy effectiveness measures, and ecological alleviation endeavors present chances to decrease natural effect.

Energy Security: Guaranteeing a safe and solid energy supply is an essential test, particularly even with fluctuating worldwide oil costs and international vulnerabilities. Energy expansion and key stores offer open doors for improving energy security.

Energy Access*: Extending energy admittance to all residents, especially in remote and underserved regions, stays a basic test. Off-network and decentralized energy arrangements, alongside last-mile availability drives, offer open doors for accomplishing widespread zap.

Foundation Investment*: The advancement of framework, including power age and transmission offices, requires significant speculation. Public-private associations, unfamiliar speculation, and inventive funding models give open doors to foundation supporting.

Innovation Adoption*: Utilizing cutting edge innovations, like savvy networks, energy capacity, and advanced framework, can upgrade the proficiency and dependability of the power area. Savvy meters and lattice incorporation innovations offer open doors for further developing energy the executives.

Electric Mobility*: The development of electric vehicles (EVs) presents both a test and an open door. EVs can lessen ozone harming substance emanations and air contamination, however their reception requires the improvement of charging foundation and arrangements that advance clean transportation.

Energy Efficiency*: Underscoring energy proficiency in enterprises, structures, and apparatuses offers open doors for diminishing energy utilization and functional expenses. Energy-proficient advancements and practices can upgrade the supportability of the power area.

3.3 The Green Revolution and its significance

The Green Unrest was a momentous period throughout the entire existence of farming and food creation, portrayed by the reception of present day innovations and practices that fundamentally expanded crop yields and changed horticulture on a worldwide scale. The Green Upset, which started during the twentieth hundred years, significantly affected agrarian efficiency, food security, and monetary advancement in nations all over the planet. This story investigates the beginnings, key parts, and extensive meaning of the Green Upheaval, both with regards to India and on a worldwide scale.

Beginnings of the Green Upheaval

The Green Unrest had its starting points during the twentieth century when the world was confronting a developing food emergency. The worldwide populace was extending quickly, and there were worries about the capacity of customary cultivating strategies to fulfill the rising need for food. This period was set apart by the cooperative endeavors of researchers, policymakers, and humanitarian associations to address these difficulties.

The Job of Norman Borlaug: Dr. Norman Borlaug, an American agronomist and plant researcher, is in many cases credited as the dad of the Green Upheaval. His work zeroed in on growing high-yielding, sickness safe wheat assortments. Borlaug's endeavors in Mexico prompted the improvement of semi-bantam wheat assortments, which could uphold heavier grain heads and were less inclined to housing (falling over). These new wheat assortments could essentially increment yields.

The Rockefeller Establishment and CIMMYT: The Rockefeller Establishment assumed a significant part in supporting Borlaug's examination and the foundation of the Global Maize and Wheat Improvement Center (CIMMYT) in Mexico. CIMMYT turned into a center for research and the improvement of further developed wheat and maize assortments.

The Indian Association: The progress of the Green Insurgency was not restricted to Mexico. In India, Dr. M.S. Swaminathan, a rural researcher, assumed a significant part in advancing the Green Upheaval. He supported the reception of high-yielding assortments (HYVs) of wheat and rice, which were instrumental in expanding food creation in India.

Key Parts of the Green Upheaval

The Green Upheaval enveloped a few vital parts and developments that added to its prosperity and importance. These parts included:

High-Yielding Assortments (HYVs): The improvement of HYVs of staple harvests, like wheat and rice, was a foundation of the Green Unrest. These new assortments had more limited development cycles, expanded protection from nuisances and illnesses, and higher grain yields.

Worked on Cultivating Practices: The Green Upset presented current cultivating works on, including the utilization of substance composts, pesticides, and herbicides. These data sources were utilized in mix with HYVs to upgrade crop efficiency.

Water system and Water The executives: The extension of water system framework was critical to the Green Transformation. Water system considered numerous trimming seasons and diminished the gamble of harvest disappointment because of dry spell. Projects like India's Bhakra-Nangal and Hirakud Dam were instrumental in growing water system.

Motorization: Automation of horticulture, including the utilization of work vehicles and other ranch hardware, further developed effectiveness and decreased the work expected for cultivating. This opened up work for other non-rural exercises.

Framework Advancement: Interests in rustic foundation, like streets, storerooms, and promoting networks, worked with the development of horticultural items from homesteads to business sectors.

Augmentation Administrations: The Green Insurgency was joined by the development of horticultural expansion administrations. These administrations gave ranchers direction on present day cultivating rehearses, bug the board, and the utilization of further developed crop assortments.

Meaning of the Green Upheaval

The Green Upheaval had sweeping importance in numerous aspects, including food security, monetary turn of events, and natural effect. Its suggestions can be surveyed in the accompanying regions:

Food Security: One of the main accomplishments of the Green Insurgency was its commitment to worldwide food security. The expanded harvest yields, especially in wheat and rice, prompted a significant ascent in food creation. This improvement assumed a critical part in tending to craving and hunger in many regions of the planet.

Expanded Farming Efficiency: The Green Upheaval decisively expanded agrarian efficiency, permitting nations to deliver more food with the equivalent or even diminished land and work inputs. This higher efficiency guaranteed a consistent food supply for developing populaces.

Financial Turn of events: The Green Upheaval essentially affected rustic economies. Expanded crop yields and pay created by ranchers animated financial improvement in provincial regions. Ranchers had more pay to spend, which helped nearby organizations and administrations.

Destitution Lightening: By raising the pay of ranchers and expanding work open doors in agribusiness, the Green Transformation added to neediness easing in provincial regions. It worked on the expectations for everyday comforts of millions of individuals.

Mechanical Development: The Green Unrest denoted a time of extraordinary mechanical development in horticulture. The improvement of HYVs, the utilization of manures, and motorization of cultivating rehearses were all spearheading advancements that changed the area.

Worldwide Effect: The progress of the Green Upset in nations like India filled in as a model for different countries confronting food security challenges. Its impact stretched out past boundaries, with nations in Asia, Latin America, and Africa embracing comparable systems to help rural creation.

Ecological Worries: While the Green Unrest had significant advantages, it likewise raised natural worries. The concentrated utilization of substance manures and pesticides prompted soil debasement, water contamination, and adverse consequences on biodiversity.

Reliance on a Couple of Harvest Assortments: The emphasis on a set number of high-yielding harvest assortments, while expanding generally creation, likewise prompted hereditary consistency in crops, making them more powerless against irritations and illnesses.

Water Scarcity*: The Green Upheaval's dependence on water system additionally added to expanded water use, which raised worries about water shortage and impractical groundwater extraction in certain districts.

The Green Unrest in India

India's involvement in the Green Upset is especially huge, given the nation's enormous and different populace, and its rural area's focal job in the economy.

Wheat and Rice*: In India, the Green Upset basically centered around wheat and rice, as these were the staple yields that could address food security concerns. The presentation of high-yielding assortments of wheat and rice prompted critical expansions underway.

Punjab and Haryana*: The provinces of Punjab and Haryana were at the very front of the Green Unrest in India. These states took on current agrarian works on, including the utilization of HYVs, water system, and substance inputs. The outcome of the Green Transformation in these states made them the "breadbasket of India."

Influence on Food Production*: The Green Unrest considerably affected food creation in India. Wheat creation expanded from 11 million tons in 1965 to 95 million tons in 2019, while rice creation rose from 35 million tons to 116 million tons during a similar period.

Strategy Support*: The Indian government assumed a fundamental part in advancing the Green Upheaval through approaches that upheld the reception of current farming practices. These arrangements remembered sponsorships for composts, interests in water system framework, and expansion administrations for ranchers.

Challenges and Concerns*: While the Green Upset in India made amazing progress in expanding food creation, it likewise raised difficulties and concerns. These included issues connected with natural maintainability, value in admittance to current data sources, and the centralization of advantages in specific areas.

Worldwide Effect and Heritage

The Green Unrest's effect was not restricted to India; it had a worldwide reach. Its prosperity filled in as a model for different nations hoping to support their farming efficiency and further develop food security. A few critical parts of the Green Upheaval's worldwide effect and heritage include:

Reception in Different Nations: The progress of the Green Upset in India propelled comparative drives in nations like Mexico, the Philippines, and numerous African countries. These endeavors intended to duplicate the Indian model and work on rural efficiency.

Innovative Exchange: The Green Upheaval included the exchange of innovation, information, and further developed crop assortments to nations confronting food security challenges. This information trade assumed a basic part in changing horticulture on a worldwide scale.

Headways in Plant Breeding*: The Green Transformation sped up progressions in plant reproducing and the improvement of high-yielding harvest assortments. These headways kept on helping farming and food creation past the Green Upset period.

Reasonable Agriculture*: The Green Upheaval's accentuation on expanding crop yields and food creation established the groundwork for the advancement of maintainable agribusiness rehearses. It featured the significance of offsetting efficiency with ecological manageability.

Mechanical Innovation*: The Green Unrest denoted a time of serious mechanical development in farming. It exhibited the capability of science and innovation to address worldwide food security challenges.

Proceeded with Challenges*: While the Green Unrest had an extraordinary effect, it likewise confronted continuous difficulties connected with ecological maintainability, value in admittance to present day inputs, and hereditary variety in crops.

Chapter 4

"The Industrial Landscape: Manufacturing and Innovation"

The modern scene of the 21st century is a complicated and dynamic embroidery of assembling and development. It is an existence where innovation and industry have become indistinguishable, shaping our lives in significant ways. The progressions in assembling cycles, materials, and advances have altered how items are planned, delivered, and appropriated. In this consistently developing scene, enterprises and organizations should adjust or risk becoming out of date.

One of the main drivers of progress in the modern scene is the fast speed of advancement. The tenacious quest for productivity, supportability, and intensity has prompted the advancement of new innovations and assembling techniques. Added substance fabricating, otherwise called 3D printing, has arisen as a unique advantage in the creation of many items, from aviation parts to redid clinical inserts. This innovation takes into consideration the formation of complicated and multifaceted plans that were already difficult to produce. Besides, it diminishes waste and energy utilization, making it an all the more harmless to the ecosystem elective.

Development isn't bound to the assembling system itself yet in addition stretches out to the actual items. Savvy fabricating has turned into a popular expression in the business, as organizations endeavor to make items that are more associated and wise. Brilliant gadgets and sensors implanted in items empower ongoing information assortment and examination, prompting better item execution and client encounters. For instance, in the car business, vehicles are presently furnished with sensors that screen different parts of the vehicle's exhibition, considering prescient upkeep and further developed wellbeing.

Supportability is one more main impetus in the modern scene. As worries about environmental change and asset consumption mount, makers are feeling the squeeze to take on additional harmless to the ecosystem rehearses. The reception of environmentally friendly power sources, for example, sun oriented and wind power, in assembling offices is turning out to be progressively normal. Moreover, the improvement of manageable materials, for example, bioplastics and reused metals, is diminishing the natural effect of assembling processes.

The globalization of supply chains has additionally changed the modern scene. Organizations are currently obtaining parts and materials from everywhere the world, exploiting cost efficiencies and particular mastery. In any case, this expanded interconnectivity likewise presents difficulties as far as store network strength. The Coronavirus pandemic uncovered weaknesses in worldwide stock chains, driving organizations to rethink their procedures and search for ways of differentiating their sources.

The labor force in the modern scene has developed too. Robotization and advanced mechanics are assuming an undeniably unmistakable part in assembling, performing assignments that were once finished by human hands. While this computerization has prompted more prominent effectiveness, it has additionally raised worries about work removal and the requirement for retraining and upskilling of the labor force. Human specialists are currently expected to team up with robots and work complex machines, requiring an alternate arrangement of abilities than customary assembling jobs.

The modern scene isn't restricted to a solitary area; it incorporates many enterprises, each with its exceptional difficulties and potential open doors. We should investigate a portion of the key areas that are molding the modern scene in the 21st hundred years.

The Aeronautic trade

The avionic business has for quite some time been at the cutting edge of mechanical development. In the 21st hundred years, it keeps on pushing the limits of what is conceivable. High level materials, like carbon composites, are being utilized to make airplane lighter and more eco-friendly. Besides, the advancement of supersonic and hypersonic airplane vows to change air travel by decreasing travel times altogether.

The aeronautic trade is likewise a trailblazer in added substance fabricating. 3D printing is utilized to create unpredictable and lightweight parts, lessening the heaviness of airplane and further developing eco-friendliness. Also, the aeronautic trade is putting resources into independent flight innovation, determined to foster self-steering airplane that can decrease human blunder and increment wellbeing.

The Car Business

The car business is going through a significant change, driven by the push for electric and independent vehicles. Electric vehicles (EVs) are turning out to be progressively well known as legislatures and purchasers focus on diminishing ozone depleting substance discharges.

Significant automakers are putting vigorously in EV innovation, fully intent on getting rid of gas powered motors.

Independent vehicles, frequently alluded to as self-driving vehicles, are likewise not too far off. These vehicles can possibly lessen mishaps and gridlock, as well as give versatility answers for the people who can't drive. Nonetheless, the improvement of independent vehicles raises complex issues connected with guideline, risk, and online protection.

The medical services and drug industry

The medical services and drug industry is another area where advancement is changing the scene. The improvement of customized medication, empowered by progresses in genomics and biotechnology, considers more exact and successful medicines. 3D printing innovation is utilized to make custom inserts and prosthetics, working on the personal satisfaction for some patients.

Telemedicine and computerized wellbeing arrangements have acquired conspicuousness, especially directly following the Coronavirus pandemic. These advancements empower remote observing and meeting, lessening the requirement for in-person visits to medical services offices. Man-made consciousness (artificial intelligence) is likewise transforming medical services, helping with analysis, drug disclosure, and patient consideration.

The energy business

The energy business is encountering a shift towards environmentally friendly power sources and supportability. Sun based and wind power are currently cutthroat with customary petroleum derivatives regarding cost, making clean energy a reasonable choice for enormous scope power age. Energy capacity innovations, like high level batteries, are fundamental for putting away sustainable power and guaranteeing a steady power supply.

The investigation of elective energy sources, for example, atomic combination, holds the commitment of giving almost boundless clean energy. Combination, if effectively tackled, could reform the manner in which we produce and consume power, with the possibility to address the world's energy needs without the downsides of atomic splitting.

The assembling scene is likewise affected by international elements. Exchange strains, duties, and inventory network disturbances have made organizations reexamine their obtaining techniques and consider reshoring or nearshoring creation. Furthermore, the protected innovation and innovation move issues are vital to the worldwide assembling scene, especially in ventures with trend setting innovation, like semiconductors and broadcast communications.

The Eventual fate of Work

As the modern scene advances, so does the idea of work. The ascent of robotization and computer based intelligence thely affects work. While robotization can further develop efficiency and diminish difficult work, it likewise raises worries about work dislodging. The labor force should adjust to the changing requests of industry and get new abilities to stay cutthroat in the gig market.

To address the difficulties representing things to come of work, states, instructive foundations, and organizations are putting resources into labor force improvement and retraining programs. Deep rooted learning is turning into a need as people should persistently refresh their abilities to stay up with innovative headways. The idea of a "fourth modern transformation" described by the combination of computerized, natural, and actual frameworks, is driving the requirement for an exceptionally versatile and well informed labor force.

Comprehensive Advancement

As the modern scene propels, it is critical to guarantee that the advantages of development are shared extensively. Comprehensive advancement looks to limit variations in admittance to innovation and open doors. It perceives that not all people and networks have equivalent admittance to schooling, assets, and the necessary resources to take part in the computerized economy.

Comprehensive development includes strategies and drives that advance variety and value in the tech and assembling areas. It additionally thinks about the moral ramifications of innovative progressions, like information protection and the mindful utilization of artificial intelligence. Inclusivity isn't just an ethical goal yet additionally an essential one, as it encourages a stronger and versatile modern scene.

The Difficulties of Online protection

With the rising digitalization of businesses, the significance of online protection couldn't possibly be more significant. The modern scene is defenseless against cyberattacks that can upset activities, compromise information, and posture dangers. Safeguarding basic framework, like power networks and transportation frameworks, is of most extreme significance.

The network protection scene is continually advancing as digital dangers become more refined. Associations should put resources into hearty network protection measures, including encryption, interruption location frameworks, and worker preparing. Joint effort between legislatures, organizations, and online protection specialists is fundamental to foster compelling techniques for guarding against digital dangers.

4.1 Growth of manufacturing industries

Producing businesses play had a vital impact in forming the monetary and mechanical scene of countries across the globe. These ventures envelop a huge range of areas, from car and aviation to drugs and hardware, and they have developed essentially throughout the long term. The development and advancement of assembling ventures are integral to financial thriving as well as have broad ramifications for work, advancement, and the general prosperity of society.

Authentic Point of view

The underlying foundations of assembling ventures can be followed back to the modern unrest in the late eighteenth and mid nineteenth hundreds of years. This period denoted a critical shift from agrarian and make based economies to motorized, large scale manufacturing frameworks.

The creation of steam motors, the automation of material creation, and the improvement of new apparatus were critical in driving this change.

The principal modern unrest established the groundwork for the development of assembling ventures by presenting advancements that expanded efficiency and decreased the expense of creation. The utilization of hardware, controlled by steam and water, prompted the foundation of processing plants, and a flood in the assembling of materials, iron, and coal mining.

The second modern upheaval, which started during the nineteenth hundred years, was portrayed by headways in the steel and synthetic ventures, the extension of the railroad organization, and the development of the phone and power. These improvements sped up industrialization as well as encouraged globalization, as merchandise could be shipped all the more proficiently across significant distances.

The twentieth century saw the third modern upheaval, driven by the ascent of gadgets and data innovation. The innovation of the semiconductor, the improvement of the web, and the development of media communications networks fundamentally changed assembling enterprises. Mechanization and computerization became key to creation processes, prompting expanded effectiveness and accuracy.

The development of assembling businesses is characteristically connected to mechanical progressions, and each modern transformation achieved an influx of development that re-imagined the assembling scene. The 21st century is set apart by the combination of advanced advancements, information examination, and man-made brainpower into assembling processes, introducing the time of Industry 4.0 or the fourth modern transformation.

Key Drivers of Development

A few variables have driven the development of assembling enterprises throughout the long term. These variables keep on forming the business' direction in the advanced period.

Mechanical Development: The determined quest for innovative development has been a main impetus behind the development of assembling businesses. From motorization to computerization, and from the appearance of PCs to the ascent of man-made brainpower, development has reliably prompted expanded efficiency, productivity, and the capacity to create complex items.

Economies of Scale: Large scale manufacturing has permitted producing businesses to accomplish economies of scale. As the volume of creation increments, per-unit costs decline, making items more reasonable for buyers. This, thus, has added to the development of assembling areas.

Globalization: The development of worldwide stockpile chains has been a huge driver of assembling development. Organizations source natural substances, parts, and completed items from different areas of the planet to exploit cost efficiencies and specific skill. This interconnectedness has driven the development of businesses like hardware and auto.

Labor force Abilities: A talented labor force is urgent for the outcome of assembling ventures. Profoundly gifted workers are expected to work complex apparatus, participate in innovative work, and adjust to advancing advancements. States and instructive organizations assume a basic part in giving preparation and schooling to fulfill the business' needs.

Capital Speculation: The development of assembling ventures frequently requires significant capital interest in apparatus, offices, and innovative work. Admittance to financing, whether through confidential venture, government support, or corporate assets, is significant for industry extension.

Administrative Climate: Government arrangements and guidelines can essentially affect fabricating businesses. Guidelines connected with natural security, wellbeing, exchange, and protected innovation, among others, shape the working climate for assembling organizations.

Key Assembling Areas

Producing enterprises envelop a wide range of areas, each with its novel qualities and importance in the worldwide economy. Here are a portion of the key assembling areas that play had a pivotal impact in driving modern development:

Auto Industry: The auto business has been at the cutting edge of assembling for more than 100 years. It includes the creation of vehicles, parts, and parts. The area has encountered critical development with the improvement of electric vehicles (EVs), independent vehicles, and high level wellbeing highlights.

Airplane business: The aeronautic trade fabricates airplane, space apparatus, and related parts. It is an innovative area with an emphasis on cutting edge materials, accuracy designing, and wellbeing. Developments in this area have prompted the creation of more productive and reasonable airplane.

Gadgets and Semiconductor Assembling: The hardware business includes the creation of shopper hardware, media communications gear, and semiconductor gadgets. This area has seen outstanding development, driven by the interest for more modest, quicker, and all the more impressive electronic items.

Drug and Biotechnology Industry: The drug and biotechnology area centers around the turn of events and assembling of medications, clinical gadgets, and biotechnological items. Propels in this industry have prompted forward leaps in medication and medical care.

Energy and Inexhaustible Assets: The energy business incorporates the development of oil, gas, and environmentally friendly power sources, for example, sunlight based, wind, and hydropower. The development of environmentally friendly power advances has changed the energy area and added to endeavors to battle environmental change.

Synthetic Assembling: The compound business delivers many synthetic substances, including modern synthetics, petrochemicals, and specialty synthetic compounds. It fills in as an establishment for different other assembling areas.

Food and Refreshment Industry: The food and drink area is liable for creating a large number of consumable items. Advancements in food handling and bundling have prompted more prominent food handling and protection.

Hardware and Gear Assembling: This area creates an assortment of modern apparatus and gear, including development apparatus, farming hardware, and assembling gear. Progresses in mechanization and digitalization have been essential in this area's development.

The Job of Assembling in Financial Development

Fabricating businesses are fundamental to monetary development and improvement in light of multiple factors:

Work Creation: Assembling is a critical wellspring of work in numerous nations. It gives occupations inside assembling offices as well as across the inventory network, including providers, merchants, and specialist organizations.

Products and Exchange: Fabricated merchandise are frequently among the top commodities of numerous countries. The creation of exportable products adds to a positive equilibrium of exchange, creating income and financial steadiness.

Development and Exploration: Assembling areas are at the cutting edge of mechanical advancement. Innovative work in assembling frequently bring about headways that overflow into different areas of the economy.

Efficiency and Proficiency: The reception of current assembling processes has prompted expanded efficiency and effectiveness. This converts into lower creation costs and further developed seriousness.

Monetary Expansion: A different assembling area gives flexibility to financial shocks and recurrent slumps. It offers open doors for expansion inside the economy, decreasing reliance on a solitary area.

Framework Improvement: The development of assembling enterprises requires the advancement of foundation, including transportation organizations, energy supply, and innovative work offices, which, thus, helps the more extensive economy.

Difficulties and Valuable open doors

While assembling ventures offer huge development potential, they likewise face various difficulties. These difficulties include:

Mechanical Interruption: The quick speed of innovative progression can make it moving for assembling organizations to keep up. Putting resources into new innovations and overhauling existing frameworks is many times an exorbitant undertaking.

Worldwide Rivalry: Makers should contend on a worldwide scale, which can prompt strain on valuing and benefit. The capacity to stay cutthroat frequently relies on development and cost-productivity.

Labor force Progress: Robotization and digitization are changing the idea of work in assembling. While they further develop proficiency, they likewise lead to work removal and require a gifted labor force equipped for working close by machines.

Ecological Supportability: Natural worries, including environmental change and asset consumption, are progressively pertinent to assembling. Meeting maintainability objectives and consenting to ecological guidelines present the two difficulties and potential open doors.

Production network Weaknesses: The Coronavirus pandemic uncovered weaknesses in worldwide stock chains. Producers are reevaluating their production network systems and investigating choices, for example, reshoring or nearshoring.

4.2 Technological innovations and their impact

The quick speed of mechanical development has been a principal trait of the 21st hundred years. Leap forwards in different fields, from data innovation to biotechnology, have changed the manner in which we live, work, and impart. These advancements affect each part of society, including the economy, medical care, schooling, and, surprisingly, how we might interpret the world. In this conversation, we will investigate probably the main mechanical advancements and their colossal impacts.

The Computerized Upheaval and Data Innovation

The computerized upheaval, portrayed by the boundless reception of advanced advances, especially PCs and the web, has been one of the most extraordinary mechanical developments within recent memory. The web, specifically, has reformed the manner in which we access and offer data, direct business, and associate with others across the globe.

The Web: The web has generally adjusted the manner in which we access and trade data. It has made information more open, empowering individuals to learn, research, and convey on an exceptional scale. The ascent of online schooling stages, open-access research, and cooperative web-based instruments has democratized learning and exploration.

Online commercial centers have changed trade, making it feasible for organizations, all things considered, to contact a worldwide crowd. Online business has turned into a trillion-dollar industry, upsetting the retail area.

Virtual Entertainment: The approach of online entertainment stages, like Facebook, Twitter, and Instagram, has had an impact on the manner in which we associate with others and consume data. These stages have reshaped individual connections as well as essentially affected political talk and social developments. They have become amazing assets for assembly, correspondence, and impact.

Large Information and Information Investigation: The expansion of advanced innovations has produced a gigantic volume of information. Huge information investigation, controlled by AI and man-made consciousness, has empowered associations to extricate important bits of knowledge from this information. This has been especially compelling in business, permitting organizations to pursue information driven choices, customize benefits, and enhance activities. It has likewise altered medical services, where information examination is utilized for determination, therapy, and medication disclosure.

Portable Innovation

Versatile innovation, including cell phones and tablets, has turned into an essential piece of current life. It has fundamentally altered the manner in which we convey, access data, and perform ordinary assignments.

Cell phones: Cell phones have developed from simple specialized gadgets to strong PCs that fit in the center of your hand. They have become irreplaceable devices for data, amusement, and efficiency. Portable applications have made whole biological systems that permit clients to perform undertakings going from banking to requesting food with a couple of taps on their screens.

Portable Installments: Versatile innovation has empowered computerized wallets and versatile installment frameworks. Applications like Apple Pay and research Pay permit clients to make installments utilizing their cell phones, lessening the requirement for actual money or Mastercards. This development has changed the manner in which we go through with monetary exchanges, making them quicker and more advantageous.

Man-made brainpower (computer based intelligence) and AI

Man-made brainpower, the advancement of PC frameworks that can perform undertakings that ordinarily require human knowledge, has taken critical steps as of late. AI, a subset of man-made intelligence, includes preparing calculations to further develop their exhibition in light of information.

Independent Vehicles: man-made intelligence and AI assume a urgent part in the improvement of independent vehicles. Organizations like Tesla and Waymo are pushing the limits of self-driving vehicles.

These vehicles can possibly upset transportation by further developing wellbeing and productivity and diminishing the requirement for individual vehicle proprietorship.

Medical services: computer based intelligence is changing medical care by aiding determination, drug revelation, and the personalization of therapy plans. AI calculations break down clinical information to distinguish examples and make expectations. Man-made intelligence controlled telemedicine stages are additionally making medical care more available, particularly in remote or underserved regions.

Proposal Frameworks: Online stages like Netflix and Amazon use computer based intelligence calculations to make customized suggestions to clients. These proposal frameworks improve the client experience as well as drive deals and commitment.

Biotechnology and Hereditary Designing

Biotechnology, especially hereditary designing, has taken astounding steps, opening up potential outcomes that were once the stuff of sci-fi.

Genome Altering: Advancements like CRISPR-Cas9 permit researchers to alter the hereditary code of life forms with accuracy. This can possibly fix hereditary infections, improve yields, and even make originator children. The moral ramifications of these innovations are a subject of continuous discussion.

Quality Treatment: Quality treatment is showing guarantee in treating beforehand serious hereditary sicknesses. It includes the presentation of utilitarian qualities into a patient's cells to address or supplant defective ones.

Environmentally friendly power and Practical Advancements

As worries about environmental change and natural manageability have developed, there has been a critical push for the improvement of environmentally friendly power sources and feasible innovations.

Sunlight based Energy: Sun oriented power has become more open and reasonable, because of progressions in sun powered charger innovation. Sun oriented establishments on housetops and sun based ranches are adding to a change to cleaner energy sources.

Electric Vehicles (EVs): The improvement of electric vehicles, for example, those delivered by Tesla and different automakers, is pushing a shift away from customary gas powered motors. EVs diminish ozone harming substance emanations and can possibly reform transportation.

Space Investigation and Business Spaceflight

Space investigation has seen a resurgence with privately owned businesses like SpaceX and Blue Beginning rivaling government organizations in pushing the limits of human presence in space.

Business Spaceflight: Privately owned businesses have entered the space race, offering the potential for space the travel industry and more reasonable admittance to space. SpaceX's reusable Hawk rockets and aggressive designs for Mars colonization have revived interest in space investigation.

Ecological Advancements

Even with developing ecological difficulties, different innovations have been created to moderate the effect of human exercises in the world.

Carbon Catch and Capacity: Advancements for catching and putting away fossil fuel byproducts from modern cycles are a work in progress. These innovations can possibly assist with relieving environmental change by diminishing ozone harming substance emanations.

Sustainable power Stockpiling: Imaginative battery advances are pivotal for the broad reception of sustainable power sources like breeze and sunlight based power. Lattice scale energy capacity frameworks, including lithium-particle batteries, are assuming a significant part in the change to clean energy.

Difficulties and Suggestions

While mechanical developments have achieved various advantages, they additionally present difficulties and suggestions that society should address.

Protection Concerns: The immense measure of information gathered and handled by computerized innovations has raised worries about individual security. Defending individual data from breaks and abuse is a continuous test.

Work Dislodging: Robotization, simulated intelligence, and mechanical technology can possibly supplant specific positions, especially those that include dreary and routine errands. Subsequently, worries about work relocation and the requirement for labor force retraining have become more noticeable.

Moral Situations: Advances, for example, hereditary designing and computer based intelligence bring up complex moral issues. The potential for creator infants and the outcomes of controlling the human genome present quandaries that require cautious thought.

Network protection: As innovation progresses, so do the capacities of cybercriminals. Safeguarding basic foundation and information from cyberattacks is a consistent fight. The potential for enormous scope cyberattacks presents critical dangers to state run administrations and organizations.

Access Incongruities: The advantages of mechanical advancements are not similarly circulated. Admittance to cutting edge innovations and computerized assets differs broadly, both inside and between nations. Tending to these variations is a squeezing concern.

Maintainability: While a few mechanical developments add to manageability, others, like the quick creation of electronic waste, present natural difficulties. Guaranteeing that innovation is created and utilized in a reasonable way is a basic thought.

Administrative and Legitimate Structures: As innovation develops, the lawful and administrative system should keep pace. Policymakers and legitimate specialists face difficulties in adjusting existing regulations to resolve issues connected with innovation, like information assurance, protected innovation, and online substance.

Last Contemplations

Mechanical advancements have reshaped our reality in significant ways. The computerized upheaval, man-made consciousness, biotechnology, sustainable power, and space investigation have all achieved tremendous changes to our regular routines and our comprehension of the world. As innovation keeps on propelling, society should wrestle with the moral, social, and ecological ramifications of these developments. Adjusting the potential for progress with the requirement for capable turn of events and impartial access is a continuous test. Eventually, the effect of mechanical advancements will rely on how they are bridled and incorporated into the texture of our social orders.

4.3 The role of public and private enterprises

Public and confidential endeavors assume unmistakable yet interconnected parts in the worldwide economy. These two areas have interesting qualities, purposes, and techniques for activity. The transaction among public and confidential endeavors is fundamental for cultural advancement, monetary development, and the arrangement of fundamental labor and products. In this conversation, we will dig into the jobs and elements of the two areas, analyzing their assets, shortcomings, and the manners in which they complete one another.

Public Endeavors:

Public endeavors, otherwise called state-possessed ventures (SOEs) or government-claimed undertakings, are elements possessed and worked by legislatures at different levels — nearby, local, or public. The fundamental goals of public ventures are much of the time molded by open arrangement and government orders.

Administration Arrangement: Public ventures are much of the time entrusted with conveying fundamental administrations to people in general. This incorporates regions like medical care, schooling, public transportation, and utilities. These administrations are viewed as principal for cultural prosperity and may not generally be productive in a simply monetary sense.

Syndication Guideline: In specific businesses, state run administrations make public undertakings to direct and control normal restraining infrastructures. There rivalry might be wasteful or hurtful to shoppers. Areas like water, power, and postal administrations frequently fall into this class. Public endeavors in these areas guarantee impartial access and sensible valuing.

Foundation Speculation: States utilize public endeavors to put resources into and keep up with basic framework, like streets, extensions, and air terminals. These substances can zero in on long haul improvement and address framework projects that probably won't be quickly productive however are fundamental for the country's development.

Monetary Adjustment: Public undertakings can be instrumental in the midst of financial emergencies. They can act as a method for states to neutralize monetary slumps by making position, invigorating interest, or offering monetary help to battling enterprises.

Strategy Execution: Public ventures are in many cases used to carry out government approaches, particularly in areas like medical services and schooling. Legislatures can apply direct command over these administrations to guarantee the satisfaction of explicit strategy objectives, like all inclusive medical care or open training.

Confidential Undertakings:

Confidential endeavors are organizations possessed and worked by people or confidential associations. They are fundamentally determined by the benefit rationale and rivalry in the commercial center. The jobs and elements of private undertakings are particular from those of public ventures:

Financial Development and Occupation Creation: Confidential undertakings are the essential motors of monetary development in many economies. They drive development, efficiency, and occupation creation. By contending on the lookout, confidential undertakings spike financial turn of events and add to a country's riches.

Proficiency and Advancement: Confidential undertakings are much of the time more proficient than their public partners because of the benefit motivation. They continually try to further develop activities, diminish costs, and improve to stay serious. This drive for proficiency benefits buyers and energizes innovative headways.

Risk-Taking and Business venture: Confidential undertakings are more ready to face challenges, contribute capital, and investigate unfamiliar business sectors. Business and development are the main impetuses behind the formation of new items, administrations, and ventures. Confidential area entertainers are instrumental in investigating new wildernesses and disturbing laid out business sectors.

Serious Business sectors: Confidential ventures flourish in aggressive conditions. Rivalry prompts lower costs, expanded quality, and more prominent customer decision. It additionally urges organizations to adjust to changing client inclinations.

Purchaser Decision: Confidential ventures offer a great many items and administrations to address customer issues and inclinations. From cell phones to dress to food, the confidential area gives different choices to people.

Reciprocal Jobs:

Public and confidential endeavors frequently cooperate to address different cultural necessities and monetary objectives. Their reciprocal jobs are clear in the accompanying ways:

Foundation Advancement: Public undertakings put resources into and keep up with basic framework, while private ventures might be associated with the development, activity, and support of public framework projects through open confidential organizations (PPPs).

Instruction and Medical care: Public endeavors frequently give schooling and medical care administrations, while private ventures might offer strengthening administrations or elective arrangements. For instance, non-public schools and medical care suppliers might offer particular administrations, adding to a more expanded instructive and medical care scene.

Public Obtainment: Legislatures depend on confidential undertakings to give labor and products to public tasks. Through agreements and tenders, confidential organizations assume a vital part in executing public works.

Innovative work: Confidential undertakings are frequently at the front of innovative work (Research and development) endeavors, yet open ventures and government organizations might support or team up with private area entertainers on projects with more extensive social or logical goals.

Work Creation and Monetary Development: Public ventures can invigorate financial development by collaborating with private organizations. Joint endeavors and coordinated efforts frequently lead to work creation and expanded financial action.

Ecological Maintainability: Public and confidential endeavors team up on manageability drives. Legislatures might set ecological guidelines and norms, while private organizations put resources into green advancements and manageable practices to meet these necessities.

Difficulties and Concerns:

While public and confidential ventures assume basic parts in financial and cultural turn of events, there are a few difficulties and concerns related with every area:

Public Endeavors:

Failure: Public undertakings can once in a while become wasteful, tormented by organization and absence of rivalry. Without the benefit rationale, they might battle to control costs and advance.

Political Impact: Public ventures can be defenseless to political obstruction, which can prompt fumble and misallocation of assets.

Monetary Limitations: Public undertakings frequently depend on government subsidizing, which can be dependent upon monetary requirements. This might restrict their capacity to fulfill public need or put resources into basic foundation.

Absence of Rivalry: In areas overwhelmed by open endeavors, there might be an absence of contest, bringing about greater costs, lower quality, and less decisions for buyers.

Confidential Undertakings:

Disparity: The quest for benefit by confidential endeavors can in some cases lead to pay imbalance and abundance focus. This has social and monetary ramifications, as it can compound inconsistencies between the rich and poor people.

Momentary Concentration: Confidential ventures might focus on transient additions over long haul supportability. This can prompt choices that augment benefits in the short run yet hurt the climate or society in the long haul.

Imposing business model and Oligopoly: In specific ventures, confidential endeavors can make syndications or oligopolies, restricting contest and customer decision. Hostile to serious way of behaving can prompt maltreatments of market power.

Natural Effect: Confidential ventures, especially in extractive enterprises, can negatively affect the climate. The quest for benefit might prompt unreasonable asset utilization and contamination.

Difficult exercise:

Finding the right harmony among public and confidential undertakings is fundamental for a well-working economy and a fair society. This equilibrium relies upon variables like the country's monetary framework, cultural qualities, and strategy targets. The suitable job of every area changes across various nations and settings.

Instances of Viable Cooperation:

A few models feature the potential for successful cooperation among public and confidential ventures:

Public-Private Associations (PPPs): PPPs are arrangements among states and confidential substances to convey public administrations or framework mutually. These associations are normal in regions like transportation (e.g., expressways), energy (e.g., public-private power plants), and medical services (e.g., secretly oversaw clinics).

Space Investigation: Legislatures team up with private ventures to propel space investigation. SpaceX, for example, has worked with NASA on different missions, including the improvement of the Group Mythical beast shuttle.

Training: Public-private associations in training include the cooperation of non-public schools, sanction schools, and schooling the executives associations. They work close by open organizations to work on the nature of training and grow access.

Medical services: State run administrations might collaborate with private medical care suppliers to extend admittance to clinical benefits or diminish sit tight times for particular therapies.

Natural Drives: Public and confidential ventures frequently team up on ecological undertakings. For instance, public guidelines may boost privately owned businesses to put resources into environmentally friendly power and economical practices.

Chapter 5

"Challenges and Milestones: Policy and Reforms"

In the present consistently developing worldwide scene, social orders and countries wrestle with a large number of difficulties, going from monetary differences and natural worries to medical services access and international strains. In the midst of this intricacy, strategies and changes assume a critical part in molding the direction of countries, tending to these difficulties, and accomplishing key achievements in friendly, monetary, and political turn of events. This article investigates the transaction of difficulties and achievements inside the domain of strategy and change, and how they impact the course of human advancement.

The world is in a condition of ceaseless change, and perhaps of the most squeezing challenge that policymakers face is staying aware of the speed of change. The computerized transformation, for example, has upset conventional enterprises, changed work showcases, and brought up issues about protection and network safety. Policymakers should adjust to these progressions quickly and insightfully, in case they fall disappointing, leaving their constituents powerless against the adverse results of fast change.

Furthermore, worldwide difficulties, for example, environmental change are reshaping the manner in which countries approach strategy and change. Environmental change represents an existential danger to our planet, and legislatures overall are wrestling with the critical need to decrease fossil fuel byproducts, progress to sustainable power sources, and relieve the impacts of a warming world. These endeavors require exhaustive approaches and changes that are powerful as well as strategically and monetarily achievable.

Medical care access is another complicated test that has expansive ramifications for social orders. The Coronavirus pandemic, which cleared across the globe, uncovered the delicacy of medical services frameworks in numerous nations and the requirement for broad changes. The pandemic required fast changes in approaches, from financing and asset portion to immunization circulation and general wellbeing drives.

Policymakers needed to explore the troublesome territory of offsetting financial interests with general wellbeing needs, all while resolving issues of immunization reluctance and deception.

Monetary incongruities are likewise an industrious test that requires nuanced strategy and change endeavors. Pay imbalance has been on the ascent in numerous nations, with a little part of the populace hoarding significant abundance while a bigger section battles to earn enough to pay the bills. Policymakers should handle this test through moderate tax assessment, social wellbeing nets, and instruction change, all of which require deft arrangement decisions.

Achievements in strategy and change frequently arise as a reaction to these difficulties. One eminent achievement is the Economical Improvement Objectives (SDGs), laid out by the Unified Countries in 2015. These 17 worldwide objectives give a thorough structure to tending to a significant number of the world's most squeezing difficulties, including destitution, disparity, environmental change, and admittance to medical services and schooling. The SDGs act as a directing light for policymakers around the world, setting clear targets and pointers for estimating progress.

Besides, achievements in innovation and development have made ready for groundbreaking arrangement changes. The approach of man-made brainpower (artificial intelligence), for example, can possibly reform ventures and administrations. Policymakers should adjust to this mechanical achievement by making guidelines that address moral worries, information protection, and the fate of work in a mechanized world.

In the domain of environment strategy, the Paris Understanding stands as a critical achievement. In 2015, nations all over the planet met up to focus on restricting an Earth-wide temperature boost to well under 2 degrees Celsius above pre-modern levels. This worldwide accord addresses an achievement in worldwide collaboration on environmental change, however the genuine test lies in accomplishing and surpassing these responsibilities through powerful strategy and change endeavors.

Achievements in medical care strategy frequently rotate around growing access and further developing results. The Reasonable Consideration Act (ACA) in the US, for instance, denoted a huge achievement in medical care change. It meant to build admittance to medical care administrations and control costs, especially for those without protection. While the ACA has gained prominent headway in extending inclusion, it keeps on confronting difficulties and discussions, featuring the continuous idea of medical services strategy change.

Financial achievements are intently attached to the more extensive monetary climate and the difficulties it presents. The Incomparable Downturn of 2008 provoked a progression of monetary and administrative changes, for example, the Dodd-Plain Money Road Change and Purchaser Security Act in the US. These achievements were driven by the need to forestall future financial emergencies and safeguard purchasers.

Notwithstanding, financial arrangement and change keep on advancing, answering moving monetary scenes and arising difficulties.

One more basic part of strategy and change is the job of administration and organizations. Compelling administration structures are fundamental for creating and executing sound strategies and accomplishing achievements. The nature of establishments and their capacity to adjust and answer difficulties enormously impacts a country's progress in resolving issues like debasement, disparity, and political steadiness.

Defilement, for example, is an unavoidable test that hampers progress in numerous nations. Policymakers should execute hostile to debasement gauges and elevate straightforwardness and responsibility to accomplish significant change around here. Achievements in enemy of debasement endeavors should be visible in the foundation of specific enemy of defilement organizations, reinforcing of informant assurance, and upgraded observing of government acquisition processes.

Political steadiness is one more basic figure accomplishing strategy achievements. Countries with solid popularity based organizations frequently have a more steady world of politics, which takes into consideration predictable strategy execution. Nonetheless, difficulties, for example, political polarization and the ascent of egalitarian developments can compromise this solidness. Policymakers should explore these difficulties and work to construct agreement to accomplish significant change.

Instruction strategy is vital to tending to financial variations and accomplishing social portability. Instruction fills in as an incredible asset for breaking the pattern of neediness and imbalance. Policymakers can carry out measures to work on the nature of training, increment admittance to advanced education, and address variations in instructive results. Accomplishing achievements in training strategy frequently includes setting focuses for proficiency rates, enlistment in essential and optional schooling, and orientation value in instruction.

Globalization is both a test and an achievement in the domain of strategy and change. The interconnectedness of the world's economies and social orders has set out new open doors and difficulties. Policymakers should explore the intricacies of exchange, movement, and social trade. Achievements in globalization strategy incorporate economic alliance, political endeavors, and worldwide collaboration to resolve issues like movement and the evacuee emergency.

Security concerns, both homegrown and worldwide, assume a huge part in forming strategy and change endeavors. In an undeniably interconnected world, issues of public safety, psychological oppression, and digital dangers require watchful approach reactions.

Policymakers should adjust the requirement for security with the insurance of common freedoms and individual opportunities. Achievements in this space frequently include the foundation of new security conventions, peaceful accords on counterterrorism, and the advancement of network safety methodologies.

The job of common society and support is vital in traveling strategy and change achievements. Grassroots developments, non-legislative associations (NGOs), and local area activism can essentially affect strategy change. Whether it's the social liberties development, the natural development, or lobbies for orientation uniformity, these developments have pushed policymakers to resolve significant issues and accomplish achievements in civil rights and balance.

The data age has changed the manner in which backing works, with web-based entertainment and online stages giving new roads to commitment and assembly. These instruments empower residents to convey, coordinate, and bring issues to light about different issues. Policymakers are progressively receptive to popular assessment and activism, perceiving the force of aggregate voices in molding strategy and change.

Challenges frequently meet and cross-over, expecting policymakers to all the while address different issues. For instance, the connection between environmental change and monetary abberations is intricate. The effect of environmental change falls lopsidedly on weak populaces, intensifying monetary imbalances. Policymakers should foster incorporated approaches and changes that battle environmental change as well as address social and financial equity.

The Coronavirus pandemic fills in as a great representation of the interconnected idea of difficulties and the requirement for comprehensive strategy reactions. The pandemic's effect reaches out past general wellbeing to monetary, instructive, and social aspects. Policymakers have needed to explore the mind boggling trap of difficulties introduced by the pandemic, going with choices that influence medical services, the economy, training, and the sky is the limit from there.

In tending to these perplexing difficulties, a critical achievement for policymakers is to embrace proof based direction. Sound approach and change endeavors ought to be grounded in thorough exploration and examination. Proof based approach making includes assessing existing strategies, directing effect evaluations, and utilizing information to illuminate navigation. This approach guarantees that strategies are powerful, proficient, and customized to the particular difficulties they expect to address.

5.1 Key policy decisions shaping industrial growth

Modern development has for some time been a critical driver of monetary improvement in countries all over the planet. The assembling and modern areas contribute altogether to work, mechanical development, and financial result. Nonetheless, modern development is definitely not a detached result of market influences; it is many times the consequence of vital strategy choices made by states. In this exposition, we will investigate the basic arrangement choices that shape modern development and their broad ramifications for society and the economy.

One of the most principal strategy choices impacting modern development is interest in foundation. Sufficient foundation, including transportation organizations, energy supply, and computerized availability, is fundamental for the effective working of ventures. Legislatures that focus on foundation advancement establish a climate where enterprises can flourish. Interests in streets, ports, rail routes, and air terminals lessen transportation costs, further develop production network proficiency, and work with the development of merchandise and individuals.

Besides, admittance to dependable and reasonable energy sources is an essential for modern turn of events. Strategy choices connected with energy foundation, for example, the development of force plants, advancement of environmentally friendly power sources, and the support of the electrical network, straightforwardly influence the modern area's capacity to productively work. In like manner, the extension of computerized foundation, including broadband web access, upholds the advanced change of enterprises, empowering more noteworthy proficiency and development.

Exchange arrangements are one more basic calculate molding modern development. State run administrations should settle on the level of receptiveness to global exchange, the idea of economic accords, and the guidelines overseeing imports and commodities. International alliances, like the North American International alliance (NAFTA) or the European Association Single Market, work with the development of labor and products across borders, empowering modern development by extending market access. Then again, protectionist measures, similar to taxes and exchange boundaries, can restrict modern extension by decreasing business sector open doors and expanding creation costs.

Besides, protected innovation (IP) strategies assume a critical part in modern development, especially in information based ventures like innovation and drugs. Choices connected with patent security, intellectual property regulations, and IP requirement influence advancement and financial turn of events. Solid IP insurances can boost innovative work, as organizations and people are guaranteed of the selective freedoms to their manifestations. Then again, excessively prohibitive IP strategies might smother development by restricting admittance to information and thoughts.

Tax assessment arrangements, including corporate duties, likewise impact modern development. Lower corporate duty rates can draw in unfamiliar direct venture and empower the development of homegrown businesses. Strategy choices to give charge motivators or allowances to innovative work (Research and development) exercises can animate advancement and development in innovation driven areas. Notwithstanding, the harmony between lessening assessments to draw in speculation and guaranteeing adequate government income to support fundamental administrations should be painstakingly thought of.

Work arrangements, like the lowest pay permitted by law regulations, aggregate dealing guidelines, and labor force improvement programs, altogether influence modern development. Choices connected with work arrangements influence creation costs, work market elements, and labor force abilities. Finding some kind of harmony between safeguarding laborers' freedoms and keeping a business-accommodating climate is difficult for policymakers. Very much created work strategies can upgrade modern development by making a talented and useful labor force while guaranteeing fair working circumstances.

Ecological strategies likewise significantly affect modern development. Choices connected with natural guidelines, discharges norms, and maintainability prerequisites impact how ventures work and advance. Severe natural strategies can drive businesses to take on cleaner advances and feasible works on, prompting long haul monetary advantages by lessening ecological corruption and moderating environmental change. Notwithstanding, policymakers should cautiously offset ecological worries with the need to keep up with modern seriousness and monetary development.

Advancement and innovation arrangements are progressively fundamental for modern development in the computerized age. Legislatures can decide to help innovative work through open financing, charge motivations, or associations with the scholarly world and the confidential area. Choices connected with development approaches influence the capacity of enterprises to make new items, cycles, and administrations, prompting seriousness and development. Interests in innovative work can bring about the development of state of the art businesses and the making of high-esteem occupations.

Training strategies assume a basic part in molding the abilities and capacities of the labor force, which, thus, impact modern development. Choices about subsidizing for instruction, educational plan, and professional preparation programs influence the quality and importance of the workforce. Powerful instruction strategies can improve the capacity of businesses to get to a thoroughly prepared labor force, encouraging development and monetary development.

Admittance to supporting is an indispensable thought for modern development. Monetary strategies, including loan fees, credit accessibility, and venture motivators, shape the speculation environment for organizations.

Low-financing costs can empower capital venture and extension, while good speculation motivations can draw in unfamiliar and homegrown venture. Well-working monetary frameworks give ventures the important money to support tasks, examination, and development.

In the time of globalization, worldwide strategies assume a crucial part in modern development. Choices in regards to enrollment in worldwide associations, support in worldwide worth chains, and arrangement with global norms all effect a country's modern scene. Global strategies can open up new business sectors, work with admittance to unfamiliar assets, and set out open doors for enterprises to grow their scope. Notwithstanding, they additionally achieve difficulties connected with contest, licensed innovation freedoms, and exchange questions that should be tended to.

Administrative strategies, crossing many regions, influence modern development. Choices connected with business enlistment, permitting, natural consistence, well-being norms, and item marking straightforwardly influence how enterprises work. A smoothed out administrative climate can lessen regulatory weights and support business development and extension. Nonetheless, administrative arrangements should likewise guarantee shopper insurance, security, and ecological manageability.

Speculation advancement approaches, including impetuses for unfamiliar and homegrown financial backers, are basic for modern development. States can decide to offer tax reductions, diminished authoritative necessities, or monetary motivating forces to draw in interest in unambiguous enterprises or locales. Venture advancement arrangements plan to establish an alluring speculation environment, empowering businesses to lay out or extend their tasks.

Framework speculation is a vital driver of modern development. Transportation framework, including streets, rail routes, ports, and air terminals, works with the development of products and individuals, diminishing transportation costs and further developing inventory network effectiveness. Energy framework, including power age and dissemination, assumes a basic part in giving dependable and reasonable energy to businesses. Advanced foundation, for example, broadband web access, upholds the computerized change of enterprises, empowering more noteworthy effectiveness and development.

Arrangements connected with modern bunches and advancement environments have acquired conspicuousness as compelling systems for modern development. States can choose to help the development of modern groups, where related enterprises and organizations gather in a geographic region. Groups make an organization impact, empowering joint effort, information sharing, and development. Advancement environments, frequently connected with innovation center points and examination focuses, center around cultivating development and business. Strategy choices to put resources into these environments can bring about the rise of high-development enterprises and imaginative arrangements.

Admittance to global business sectors is fundamental for modern development. Exchange strategies, remembering choices for economic deals and taxes, straightforwardly impact a country's admittance to unfamiliar business sectors. International alliances, like the Exhaustive and Moderate Arrangement for Transoceanic Association (CPTPP) or the European Association Single Market, open up open doors for businesses to grow their span and access new clients. On the other hand, protectionist measures, like duties and exchange boundaries, can restrict modern development by confining business sector access and expanding creation costs.

A steady and unsurprising legitimate and administrative system is essential for modern development. Legitimate arrangements that guarantee the insurance of property freedoms, agreements, and licensed innovation establish a climate where organizations can work with certainty. Strategies connected with debate goal components, like mediation, likewise assume a critical part in guaranteeing a fair and productive legitimate climate for ventures. Moreover, steady and straightforward guidelines add to an anticipated business climate that draws in speculation and empowers modern extension.

5.2 The era of planned economies

The idea of arranged economies plays had a conspicuous impact in the financial and political history of the twentieth 100 years. An arranged economy, frequently connected with communist or socialist belief systems, is described by a focal power, normally the public authority, pursuing choices in regards to asset portion, creation, and circulation of labor and products. While arranged economies have been carried out with fluctuating levels of progress and in various structures, they have made a huge imprint on the worldwide monetary scene. In this exposition, we will dig into the period of arranged economies, analyzing their beginnings, key elements, difficulties, and heritages.

Beginnings and Philosophical Establishments

The underlying foundations of arranged economies can be followed back to different authentic forerunners, with their improvement impacted by a combination of communist, communist, and idealistic standards. One of the earliest defenders of arranged economies was the French logician Charles Fourier, who in the mid nineteenth century imagined a general public coordinated into phalansteries where work, utilization, and relaxation were fastidiously wanted to dispense with destitution and social disparity. Fourier's thoughts were subsequently developed by scholars, for example, Henri de Holy person Simon and Robert Owen, who advanced mutual living and the fair dissemination of assets.

The basic works of Karl Marx and Friedrich Engels laid the hypothetical basis for the more organized arranged economies of the twentieth 100 years. Marx's "Das Kapital" and "The Socialist Declaration" investigated the idea of a ridiculous society where the method for creation were on the whole claimed and controlled. As per Marx, the progress from free enterprise to socialism required a time of communism, described by unified wanting to rearrange riches and assets. These thoughts gave the scholarly establishment to the arranged economies that arose in the mid twentieth hundred years.

The Russian Transformation of 1917, drove by Vladimir Lenin and the Trotskyite Party, denoted a critical crossroads throughout the entire existence of arranged economies. The Trotskyites ousted the Temporary Government, and Lenin's administration set off to make a communist state in Russia. The ensuing development of the Soviet Association in 1922, supported by communist Leninist philosophy, acquainted the world with the idea of an arranged, midway controlled economy. The Soviet model filled in as a layout for different nations, especially in the communist coalition of Eastern Europe and Asia, which embraced arranged economies for of accomplishing social and monetary change.

Key Elements of Arranged Economies

Arranged economies are portrayed by a few unmistakable elements, which separate them from market-situated economies. The essential perspectives include:

Unified Arranging: The sign of arranged economies is focal financial preparation, normally led by a state authority, to facilitate creation, asset portion, and monetary exercises. The focal arranging authority defines objectives, assigns assets, and chooses what, how, and for whom labor and products will be created. This degree of centralization separates arranged economies from market economies where choices are fundamentally decentralized and driven by market interest.

Aggregate Possession: Arranged economies frequently underline aggregate or state responsibility for method for creation, including industrial facilities, land, and assets. In such frameworks, confidential proprietorship is either negligible or non-existent, and the state expects a predominant job in possession and control.

Value Controls: Costs in arranged economies are in many cases constrained by the public authority, with an emphasis on balancing out the expense of fundamental labor and products. Cost controls expect to check expansion, forestall cost gouging, and guarantee moderateness. Be that as it may, they can likewise prompt deficiencies and contortions in asset allotment.

Full Business: A shared objective in arranged economies is to accomplish full work. The public authority intercedes to make occupations and lessen joblessness through open works projects, recruiting motivations, and different measures.

Pay Reallocation: Decreasing pay imbalance is a critical goal in arranged economies. Strategies, for example, moderate tax collection and social government assistance programs intend to rearrange riches and give a wellbeing net to the less lucky.

State-Offered Types of assistance: Arranged economies frequently highlight broad state-offered types of assistance, including medical care, schooling, and social government assistance. The public authority assumes a focal part in guaranteeing admittance to these administrations.

Absence of Purchaser Decision: Focal arranging can restrict customer decision, as creation choices are made by the state in light of seen needs. This can prompt normalized, less different labor and products.

Long haul Arranging: Arranged economies are known for their drawn out point of view in financial preparation. The public authority frequently puts forth long term plans and objectives to direct asset distribution and creation targets.

State Control of Unfamiliar Exchange: The state regularly controls unfamiliar exchange and cash trade in arranged economies. Products and imports are dependent upon government endorsement and coordination.

Difficulties and Evaluates

The period of arranged economies was set apart by striking accomplishments, especially in industrialization, schooling, and medical care. In any case, it additionally confronted huge difficulties and studies, some of which eventually prompted the downfall of arranged economies in many regions of the planet. Key difficulties and reactions include:

Asset Allotment Failure: Focal preparation, while expected to guarantee effective asset portion, frequently prompted shortcomings. Administrative navigation, absence of market criticism, and data holes could bring about overproduction, deficiencies, or the misallocation of assets.

Absence of Development: Pundits contended that arranged economies smothered advancement and mechanical advancement. The shortfall of contest and market motivating forces could discourage inventive and pioneering drives.

Defilement and Organization: Concentrated arranging was powerless to debasement, as choices were much of the time made by a little gathering of government authorities. Administrative formality and shortcoming were normal issues.

Deficiencies and Excesses: Arranged economies habitually battled with deficiencies of fundamental merchandise and overflows of undesirable items. The absence of market components to flag market interest awkward nature added to these issues.

Disparity and Political Restraint: Regardless of the objective of decreasing pay imbalance, arranged economies frequently had strong political elites who delighted in honors not accessible to everyone. Contradict was frequently smothered, and political opportunities were limited.

Absence of Customer Decision: The restricted assortment of labor and products accessible in arranged economies was viewed as a critical downside. Buyers had less options, and item quality could endure.

Ecological Disregard: A few arranged economies ignored natural worries, bringing about contamination and asset consumption. The emphasis on quick industrialization at times came to the detriment of supportability.

Reliance on Focal Preparation: Arranged economies made a reliance on focal preparation, making it trying to progress to showcase situated frameworks when wanted.

The Breakdown of Arranged Economies

The downfall of arranged economies in the late twentieth century was driven by a blend of interior and outer variables. The disintegration of the Soviet Association in 1991 denoted a huge defining moment throughout the entire existence of arranged economies. A few Eastern European nations likewise changed away from midway arranged frameworks, embracing market-situated changes.

Interior elements included financial stagnation, failure, and an absence of buyer decision, which dissolved public help for arranged economies. Remotely, the finish of the Virus War and the launch of worldwide business sectors presented arranged economies to new monetary models and political belief systems. The advancement of exchange and the spread of neoliberal financial strategies added to the downfall of midway arranged frameworks.

China stands apart as a special case for this pattern. While it at first embraced an arranged economy under Mao Zedong, it progressively presented market-situated changes under Deng Xiaoping's initiative, bringing about noteworthy financial development and change.

5.3 The economic reforms of the 1990s and their impact

The 1990s denoted a critical defining moment in the worldwide monetary scene, with numerous nations undertaking extensive financial changes. These changes, frequently portrayed by terms like advancement, liberation, and privatization, meant to change economies that were troubled by failures, protectionism, and state control into more market-situated frameworks. The effect of these monetary changes was significant, affecting financial development, neediness decrease, globalization, and monetary steadiness. In this exposition, we will investigate the financial changes of the 1990s and their multi-layered influence on nations and the world economy.

Beginnings and Inspirations

The monetary changes of the 1990s can be followed back to a few interrelated variables and improvements. One of the essential impetuses was the finish of the Virus War and the disintegration of the Soviet Association. This international shift established a climate in which numerous nations, especially in Eastern Europe and the previous Soviet coalition, tried to progress from arranged economies to showcase situated frameworks. The breakdown of socialism, represented by the fall of the Berlin Wall in 1989, achieved a flood of progression and market changes.

One more key driver of financial changes was the acknowledgment of the impediments of protectionist and state-controlled monetary models. Numerous nations observed that their economies were troubled by inordinate guidelines, wasteful state-possessed ventures, and high exchange boundaries. These circumstances thwarted development, deterred unfamiliar speculation, and brought about monetary stagnation.

Moreover, the 1980s had seen the ascent of neoliberal financial hypotheses, which upheld for insignificant government mediation, market-arranged approaches, and the significance of rivalry. This scholarly shift fundamentally affected policymakers, who considered monetary progression to be a way to success.

The Global Money related Asset (IMF) and the World Bank assumed a focal part in upholding and supporting monetary changes. In return for monetary help, these organizations frequently expected acquiring nations to execute underlying change programs, which included measures like financial discipline, exchange progression, and privatization. While these projects were met with analysis for their social and financial results, they assumed a part in propelling business sector situated changes.

Key Parts of Financial Changes

The financial changes of the 1990s included a scope of measures pointed toward changing and rebuilding economies. A portion of the vital parts of these changes included:

Exchange Progression: Diminishing exchange boundaries, like levies and import portions, to advance worldwide exchange and increment market access for homegrown and unfamiliar organizations. This prompted an expansion in worldwide exchange and monetary reconciliation.

Liberation: Diminishing unofficial laws and administration in different areas, including money, media communications, and transportation, to advance contest, decrease failures, and improve financial dynamism.

Privatization: Moving state-possessed ventures and resources for the confidential area through different strategies, including deals, sales, and public contributions. Privatization intended to increment effectiveness and decrease the weight on government spending plans.

Monetary Discipline: Carrying out mindful financial approaches, like decreasing spending plan shortages and controling expansion, to balance out economies and draw in venture.

Money related Approach Changes: Improving national bank freedom and embracing more market-arranged financial strategies to keep up with cost soundness and energize unfamiliar speculation.

Monetary Area Changes: Modernizing and changing the monetary area by presenting market-based instruments, for example, loan cost advancement and the privatization of state-possessed banks.

Work Market Changes: Executing measures to increment work market adaptability, which frequently included changes to work regulations and guidelines to advance work creation and decrease joblessness.

Property Privileges and Law and order: Reinforcing overall sets of laws, property freedoms, and agreement implementation to give a safer climate to venture and financial action.

Influence on Monetary Development

One of the most critical and quick effects of the monetary changes of the 1990s was on financial development. Advancement and market-arranged approaches added to higher paces of financial extension in numerous nations. By diminishing exchange boundaries, organizations accessed bigger business sectors, both locally and globally. This development of market access prodded expanded creation, more noteworthy effectiveness, and improved seriousness.

Liberation and privatization likewise assumed a fundamental part in animating financial development. By decreasing state control and empowering rivalry, these changes prompted more effective asset designation and further developed efficiency. The privatization of state-possessed ventures frequently brought about expanded effectiveness, as confidential proprietorship boosted benefit chasing and development.

Monetary area changes, including loan cost advancement, extended admittance to capital and credit, empowering organizations to put resources into extension and development. The reinforcing of property freedoms and law and order gave a safer climate to venture, which pulled in both homegrown and unfamiliar capital.

China's monetary changes, started in the last part of the 1970s yet advancing during the 1990s, give a striking illustration of the effect of these strategies. The shift from a midway arranged economy to a more market-situated framework prompted momentous financial development, changing China into a worldwide monetary force to be reckoned with.

Notwithstanding, it is essential to take note of that the effect of financial changes on development differed starting with one country then onto the next. Achievement relied upon different variables, including the profundity and consistency of changes, the nature of foundations, and the worldwide financial climate.

Influence on Destitution Decrease

While the monetary changes of the 1990s prodded financial development, their effect on neediness decrease was more perplexing and frequently likely to discuss. From one perspective, the extension of monetary open doors and expanded work creation brought about better expectations for everyday comforts for some individuals. More elevated levels of monetary development were related with diminished destitution rates in a few nations.

Nonetheless, the effect on neediness was not uniform, and at times, destitution expanded. The fast progression of certain economies prompted work disengagement, especially in customary and less cutthroat enterprises. Work market changes some of the time decreased professional stability and laborers' bartering power, influencing wages and working circumstances. Social security nets were not generally strong enough to moderate the adverse results of monetary rebuilding.

Generally speaking, the financial changes were executed without even a trace of a far reaching social wellbeing net, which allowed weak populaces to be uncovered to monetary shocks. Subsequently, pundits contended that the changes frequently prompted expanded pay imbalance and social abberations.

The Asian monetary emergency of 1997-1998 fills in as a critical illustration of the intricacies of financial changes. While the emergency incited a few nations to take on additional progression and rebuilding measures, it likewise uncovered the weakness of monetary areas and the expected social expenses of quick progression.

Influence on Globalization

The monetary changes of the 1990s fundamentally added to globalization, as they prompted expanded worldwide exchange and venture. By decreasing exchange obstructions and working with market access, nations turned out to be more coordinated into the worldwide economy. Worldwide inventory chains extended, and global exchange streams flooded.

China's reconciliation into the worldwide economy, driven by financial changes and its promotion to the World Exchange Association (WTO) in 2001, represents this pattern. China's rise as the world's production line and its job as a vital participant in worldwide exchange were impacted by these changes. Likewise, India's monetary progression during the 1990s extended its job in the worldwide administrations area, especially in data innovation and business process re-appropriating.

The globalization of money was one more sign of this period. Monetary advancement and the facilitating of capital controls prompted expanded cross-line capital streams. Worldwide monetary business sectors turned out to be more interconnected, adding to the exchange of monetary emergencies across borders.

While globalization achieved open doors for financial development and advancement, it additionally raised difficulties connected with monetary solidness, pay disparity, and political strains. The Asian monetary emergency, the worldwide monetary emergency of 2008, and worries about work and ecological guidelines in worldwide stockpile chains featured a portion of these difficulties.

Influence on Monetary Security

The progression of monetary areas and expanded worldwide capital streams additionally had huge ramifications for monetary solidness. While these changes added to the development of monetary business sectors and expanded admittance to capital, they likewise presented gambles.

In a few cases, monetary progression prompted over the top loaning, speculative air pockets, and impractical credit blasts. These patterns, thus, added to monetary emergencies. The Asian monetary emergency of 1997-1998, the Russian monetary emergency of 1998, and the Argentine monetary emergency of 2001 were completely connected to weaknesses made by monetary progression.

The worldwide monetary emergency of 2008 filled in as a reminder in regards to the dangers related with ineffectively managed monetary business sectors. The emergency, set off by the breakdown of Lehman Siblings, uncovered the interconnectedness of worldwide monetary establishments and the difficulties of overseeing fundamental gamble.

Chapter 6

"Global Aspirations: Liberalization and Globalization"

The late twentieth and mid 21st hundreds of years have seen a noteworthy change in the worldwide financial scene. The main thrust behind this change has been the twin cycles of advancement and globalization. Advancement includes decreasing state mediation and guideline in the economy, cultivating contest, and empowering market-situated strategies. Globalization, then again, alludes to the rising interconnectedness of the world through exchange, venture, data streams, and social trade. These cycles have formed the world's monetary design as well as affected legislative issues, society, and culture. In this paper, we will investigate the aspects, difficulties, and effects of progression and globalization on a worldwide scale.

The Ascent of Progression

The foundations of advancement can be followed back to the financial speculations of old style progressivism, which arose in the eighteenth and nineteenth hundreds of years. Financial specialists like Adam Smith and David Ricardo contended for negligible government mediation in monetary undertakings, underlining the job of unrestricted economies in advancing financial development and individual opportunity. In any case, it was in the last 50% of the twentieth century that progression turned into a characterizing component of financial strategy, supported by a few elements and improvements.

One of the vital occasions that added to the ascent of advancement was the disappointment of focal preparation and state-controlled economies in many regions of the planet. The breakdown of the Soviet Association in 1991 denoted a defining moment, ruining the communist monetary model and encouraging the defenders of market-situated strategies. Numerous nations, especially in Eastern Europe and Asia, started financial changes pointed toward lessening state control, encouraging rivalry, and embracing private venture.

The domination of neoliberal monetary speculations assumed a significant part in propelling progression. Financial analysts like Friedrich Hayek, Milton Friedman, and James Buchanan upheld for restricted government intercession, liberation, and market-arranged approaches. These thoughts acquired conspicuousness during the late twentieth hundred years and fundamentally affected policymakers and political pioneers.

Global establishments, including the Worldwide Money related Asset (IMF) and the World Bank, assumed an instrumental part in advancing progression. In return for monetary help, these associations frequently expected acquiring nations to carry out primary change programs, which included measures like exchange advancement, privatization, and financial discipline. While these projects were met with analysis for their social and monetary outcomes, they were vital to the worldwide spread of progression.

Aspects of Advancement

Progression incorporates different aspects, with key components that impact monetary, political, and social elements. A portion of the essential components of progression include:

Exchange Progression: Lessening exchange boundaries, like taxes and import amounts, to advance worldwide exchange and market access. Exchange progression has prompted an expansion in worldwide exchange and financial coordination.

Liberation: Diminishing unofficial laws and organization in different areas, including money, media communications, and transportation, to advance rivalry, lessen shortcomings, and improve financial dynamism.

Privatization: Moving state-possessed endeavors and resources for the confidential area through strategies like deals, sales, and public contributions. Privatization means to increment effectiveness and diminish the weight on government spending plans.

Financial Discipline: Carrying out dependable monetary arrangements, like diminishing spending plan shortfalls and checking expansion, to settle economies and draw in venture.

Money related Approach Changes: Improving national bank autonomy and taking on more market-situated financial strategies to keep up with cost steadiness and empower unfamiliar venture.

Monetary Area Changes: Modernizing and changing the monetary area by presenting market-based components, for example, loan cost progression and the privatization of state-possessed banks.

Work Market Changes: Carrying out measures to increment work market adaptability, which frequently incorporates changes to work regulations and guidelines to advance work creation and diminish joblessness.

Property Privileges and Law and order: Reinforcing general sets of laws, property freedoms, and agreement implementation to give a safer climate to speculation and financial action.

Receptiveness to Unfamiliar Venture: Empowering unfamiliar direct speculation (FDI) through arrangements that ease limitations, work on endorsement processes, and give impetuses to draw in abroad capital.

Decrease of State Control: Lessening state proprietorship and control in different areas, empowering private business venture, and cultivating rivalry.

These components of advancement have been embraced to changing degrees by various nations, prompting unmistakable strategy draws near. In any case, it is critical to perceive that progression is definitely not a one-size-fits-all cycle; it happens inside the setting of every country's novel financial, political, and social conditions.

Difficulties and Investigates of Progression

While progression has yielded huge advantages, it has likewise confronted difficulties and reactions, some of which have powered continuous discussions with respect to the harmony between market-situated strategies and social government assistance. Key difficulties and evaluates of progression include:

Pay Disparity: Pundits contend that advancement can intensify pay imbalance. Quick financial development and the privatization of state resources can help the richer sections of society more than poor people, prompting more noteworthy abberations in pay and abundance.

Social Security Nets: The quest for monetary discipline and the decrease of government mediation now and again come to the detriment of social wellbeing nets. Lacking wellbeing nets can allow weak populaces to be uncovered to financial shocks and difficulties.

Natural Supportability: Progression can once in a while focus on monetary development to the detriment of ecological maintainability. Liberation and decreased government oversight might bring about lacking natural assurances and negative environmental results.

Reliance on Worldwide Business sectors: Economies that vigorously rely upon worldwide business sectors might be defenseless against outside shocks, as seen during the worldwide monetary emergency of 2008. Overreliance on send out drove development can allow nations to be uncovered to global financial changes.

Loss of State Control: The decrease of state control in essential areas, like energy, media communications, and money, can raise worries about public power and security. Some contend that unreasonable privatization can leave countries helpless against unfamiliar interests.

Social Effect: Work market changes and expanded work market adaptability can bring about work frailty and decreased specialist bartering power. Pundits fight that these progressions can prompt unfortunate working circumstances and pay stagnation.

Monetary Emergencies: Monetary advancement has been related with expanded monetary shakiness and the gamble of monetary emergencies. Fast capital inflows and surges can disturb monetary business sectors and lead to money debasements.

Influence on Neighborhood Organizations: Progression can now and then weakness nearby organizations, especially little and medium-sized endeavors (SMEs), while contending with bigger, more settled global companies.

Worldwide Stock Chains: The globalization of creation and supply chains, driven by progression, can bring about moral and natural worries connected with work rehearses, common freedoms, and environmental effects.

It is critical to take note of that the effect of advancement is setting explicit and relies upon different variables, including the profundity and consistency of changes, the nature of establishments, and the worldwide financial climate.

The Appearance of Globalization

While advancement has reshaped homegrown financial arrangements, globalization has re-imagined the worldwide monetary scene. Globalization alludes to the rising interconnectedness of the world through cross-line streams of merchandise, administrations, capital, data, and individuals. The course of globalization has been driven by different powers and improvements, which have changed the manner in which countries direct business, convey, and collaborate on a worldwide scale.

Aspects of Globalization

Globalization incorporates a few aspects, every one of which has added to its diverse nature. A portion of the vital elements of globalization include:

Exchange and Monetary Incorporation: The development of global exchange, supply chains, and the development of local financial alliances, like the European Association and the Relationship of Southeast Asian Countries (ASEAN).

Unfamiliar Direct Speculation (FDI): The rising progression of capital across borders, with worldwide companies (MNCs) laying out activities in different nations.

Data Innovation: The appearance of the web and advances in correspondence innovation have worked with the quick trade of data and changed business activities, schooling, and worldwide network.

Social Trade: The scattering of culture, values, and thoughts across borders through media, amusement, and worldwide correspondence.

Relocation: The development of individuals across borders for work, instruction, and different reasons.

Natural Reliance: The acknowledgment that ecological issues, for example, environmental change and biodiversity misfortune, are worldwide difficulties that require global collaboration.

Worldwide Stock Chains: The advancement of mind boggling creation networks that length numerous nations and districts, empowering savvy assembling and appropriation.

6.1 India's journey towards globalization

The narrative of India's excursion towards globalization is a story of change, spreading over many years and enveloping significant changes in the monetary, political, and social texture of the country. From the beginning of freedom in 1947 to the present, India has crossed a mind boggling way set apart by monetary changes, strategy movements, and combination into the worldwide economy. This excursion has been described by the two difficulties and accomplishments, and it offers important experiences into the elements of globalization in a different and quickly developing country.

Post-Freedom Monetary Arrangements

At the hour of India's freedom in 1947, the country embraced a blended economy model, impacted by communist beliefs. The public authority assumed a predominant part in financial preparation and control, with state proprietorship and guideline of key ventures. The strategy approach, known as the "Permit Raj," was described by broad administration, protectionism, and weighty limitations on confidential endeavor.

The key goals were to accomplish confidence, lessen neediness, and advance civil rights. India's most memorable Top state leader, Jawaharlal Nehru, accentuated the significance of public area undertakings and state arranging. The period saw the foundation of the Mahalanobis Model, a financial improvement methodology that expected to focus on weighty industry and diminish pay abberations.

The Monetary Emergency of 1991

By the last part of the 1980s, India's economy was confronting critical difficulties. The Permit Raj had prompted failures, an absence of seriousness, and a thriving monetary deficiency. The nation was wrestling with an equilibrium of installments emergency, and its unfamiliar trade holds were lessening. The circumstance required a reexamination of monetary strategies and a shift towards progression and globalization.

In 1991, India confronted a basic point. The public authority, drove by Head of the state P. V. Narasimha Rao and Money Clergyman Dr. Manmohan Singh, started a progression of monetary changes that noticeable a defining moment in India's excursion towards globalization. These changes were established in the accompanying key standards:

Exchange Progression: Decreasing exchange hindrances, like levies and import quantities, to advance global exchange and further develop market access.

Liberation: Facilitating unofficial laws and lessening organization to encourage contest, upgrade proficiency, and animate financial dynamism.

Privatization: Moving state-claimed endeavors to the confidential area to increment productivity and decrease the weight on government financial plans.

Financial Discipline: Carrying out capable monetary arrangements, including diminishing spending plan shortages and controling expansion, to balance out the economy and draw in speculation.

Financial Arrangement Changes: Upgrading national bank freedom and taking on more market-situated money related approaches to keep up with cost strength and energize unfamiliar speculation.

Monetary Area Changes: Modernizing and changing the monetary area by presenting market-based systems, for example, loan fee advancement and the privatization of state-claimed banks.

Worldwide Joining: Embracing globalization by empowering unfamiliar speculation and exchange to extend admittance to worldwide business sectors.

These changes, all in all known as the New Monetary Strategy, introduced another period of financial receptiveness, proclaiming India's excursion towards globalization.

Financial Changes and Globalization

The monetary changes of 1991 established the groundwork for India's combination into the worldwide economy. The changes meant to destroy exchange boundaries, advance rivalry, and empower unfamiliar speculation. The excursion towards globalization unfurled on a few fronts:

1. **Exchange and Product Development**

   One of the quick effects of advancement was the extension of India's exchange and commodity areas. Tax decreases and the expulsion of exchange limitations made Indian merchandise more aggressive in worldwide business sectors. India's commodities developed consistently, determined by enterprises like data innovation (IT), materials, and drugs. The IT and programming administrations area, specifically, experienced noteworthy development, moving India to the cutting edge of the worldwide innovation industry.

2. **Unfamiliar Direct Venture (FDI)**

   The advancement of FDI guidelines and the facilitating of passage boundaries pulled in unfamiliar financial backers to India. Areas like broadcast communications, retail, and money bit by bit opened up to unfamiliar venture. Unfamiliar organizations laid out tasks in India, bringing capital, innovation, and business potential open doors. The inundation of FDI added to financial development and innovation move.

3. **Administrations Area Development**

   The administrations area, particularly IT and business process reevaluating (BPO), arose as a significant driver of India's globalization. India's informed labor force, capability in English, and savvy work made it a favored objective for worldwide organizations looking to re-appropriate different administrations. This area made large number of occupations, expanded send out incomes, and assumed a critical part in India's mix into the worldwide economy.

4. **Monetary Coordination**

   Monetary area changes, including the progression of loan fees and the passage of private area banks, modernized India's monetary framework. The nation's securities exchanges, for example, the Bombay Stock Trade (BSE) and the Public Stock Trade (NSE), saw significant development, drawing in both homegrown and unfamiliar financial backers. India's capital business sectors turned out to be progressively incorporated with worldwide monetary business sectors.

5. **Modern and Innovative Headways**

Globalization prodded modern development, especially in areas like drugs, auto, and assembling. Cooperation with worldwide firms, admittance to trend setting innovation, and support in worldwide stock chains improved the abilities of Indian ventures. India's car area, for instance, saw the section of worldwide makers, prompting the creation of a-list vehicles.

Difficulties and Intricacies

While India's excursion towards globalization has yielded significant advantages, it has not been without its portion of difficulties and intricacies. A portion of the major questions that India has wrestled with include:

1. **Pay Imbalance and Local Differences**

   Globalization has prompted huge pay differences in India. While it has set out abundance and open doors in metropolitan habitats and high-development areas, provincial regions have not benefited similarly. Local variations in pay and improvement continue, representing a test for comprehensive development.

2. **Social Government assistance and Disparity**

   The quest for financial progression some of the time came to the detriment of social government assistance. Lacking security nets and restricted admittance to medical care and instruction have allowed weak populaces to be uncovered to monetary shocks. Pay imbalance has additionally raised worries about friendly abberations.

3. **Natural Manageability**

   As India's economy has developed, so has its natural impression. Quick industrialization, expanded energy utilization, and urbanization have presented ecological difficulties, including air and water contamination, deforestation, and the exhaustion of regular assets. Offsetting financial development with ecological maintainability stays a complicated undertaking.

4. **Administrative Difficulties**

   While advancement expected to diminish unofficial laws, it has additionally uncovered administrative difficulties in different areas, including medical services, natural assurance, and work regulations. The requirement for compelling guidelines to offset monetary development with social and ecological contemplations is a continuous concern.

5. **Political and International Intricacies**

   India's commitment with the worldwide economy has presented new components of political and international intricacies. The nation should explore worldwide exchange dealings, licensed innovation freedoms issues, and strategic difficulties connected with financial organizations.

6. **Training and Expertise Advancement**

The development of the IT and administrations area has highlighted the requirement for a talented labor force. India faces the test of upgrading its schooling and expertise improvement frameworks to satisfy the needs of a globalized economy.

Flexibility and Variation

India's excursion towards globalization has shown flexibility and versatility. The nation has endured worldwide financial emergencies, exchange debates, and international pressures while proceeding to draw in venture and extend its worldwide impression.

The Coronavirus pandemic represented an exceptional test, influencing the worldwide economy and disturbing stockpile chains. India, as a significant drug and immunization maker, assumed a vital part in tending to the pandemic. The emergency additionally incited India to speed up advanced change, online business reception, and telemedicine administrations, displaying the country's capacity to adjust to new worldwide real factors.

6.2 Opening up to foreign investment and trade

The method involved with opening up to unfamiliar speculation and exchange has been an essential driver of monetary development, improvement, and globalization for some countries all over the planet. Nations that decide to embrace this approach can encounter significant advantages, like expanded financial movement, work creation, innovative trade, and admittance to worldwide business sectors. In any case, the choice to open up to unfamiliar speculation and exchange is a perplexing and complex one, and its execution includes various contemplations and strategy decisions. This article investigates the idea of opening up to unfamiliar venture and exchange, its fundamental standards, possible advantages, and the different difficulties and intricacies included.

The Idea of Opening Up

Opening up to unfamiliar venture and exchange alludes to a nation's readiness and capacity to draw in with the worldwide economy by permitting unfamiliar substances to put resources into homegrown endeavors, partake in exchange, and lay out a presence in the homegrown market. This idea is established in the more extensive monetary way of thinking of financial progression and globalization, stressing the evacuation of exchange obstructions and the making of a more open and interconnected worldwide economy.

Key Standards of Opening Up to Unfamiliar Speculation and Exchange

The choice to open up to unfamiliar speculation and exchange is directed by a few key standards:

Near Benefit: One of the focal standards is the idea of similar benefit. This hypothesis, created by David Ricardo, proposes that nations ought to spend significant time in delivering labor and products in which they enjoy a similar benefit, and afterward exchange with different countries for labor and products which they are less proficient.

This specialization and exchange can prompt more noteworthy by and large monetary effectiveness and expanded worldwide government assistance.

Unrestricted economy Standards: Opening up to unfamiliar speculation and exchange depends on the standards of unregulated economies, where organic market decide costs, asset assignment, and monetary results. Decreasing government mediation and exchange limitations is in many cases considered to be fundamental for cultivating open business sectors.

Monetary Development and Improvement: The essential objective of opening up to unfamiliar venture and exchange is to advance financial development and advancement. Expanded worldwide exchange and venture can animate financial action, make occupations, and work on expectations for everyday comforts. For emerging nations, it very well may be a pathway to industrialization and neediness decrease.

Innovative Trade: Drawing in with unfamiliar financial backers and exchanging accomplices can work with the exchange of innovation and information. Trend setting innovations and administrative practices from created nations can assist with supporting efficiency and advancement in beneficiary nations.

Admittance to Worldwide Business sectors: An open economy furnishes homegrown organizations with admittance to a more extensive client base. Trade open doors empower organizations to grow and expand their business sectors, possibly prompting expanded deals and benefits.

Broadening and Hazard Alleviation: Expanding monetary connections and exchange accomplices can decrease the dangers related with financial slumps or political precariousness in one area or country.

Advantages of Opening Up to Unfamiliar Venture and Exchange

Opening up to unfamiliar venture and exchange can yield a large number of advantages for nations that decide to embrace this methodology:

Financial Development: Improved exchange and speculation can help monetary development, as it gives new business sectors to homegrown items and energizes interest in different areas.

Work Creation: Expanded financial action coming about because of unfamiliar venture and exchange can prompt work creation, diminishing joblessness and further developing occupations.

Mechanical Headway: Coordinated effort with unfamiliar elements opens nations to cutting edge innovations, advancement, and best practices, which can improve homegrown efficiency and modern capacities.

Admittance to Capital: Unfamiliar speculation can get genuinely necessary money to support projects, invigorate monetary exercises, and fuel business.

Broadening: Extending exchange and venture connections differentiates a country's financial base, diminishing reliance on a solitary market or industry.

Unfamiliar Trade Profit: Sending out labor and products creates unfamiliar trade income, which can be utilized for imports and global obligation overhauling.

Shopper Advantages: Customers frequently benefit from lower costs and expanded decisions for labor and products, as rivalry from unfamiliar makers can drive down costs and further develop item quality.

Foundation Advancement: Unfamiliar venture frequently incorporates projects that further develop framework, like streets, ports, and utilities, which can have positive overflow consequences for the economy.

Worldwide Mix: Receptiveness to unfamiliar speculation and exchange associates nations with worldwide worth chains, permitting them to turn out to be important for global creation organizations.

Difficulties and Intricacies

While opening up to unfamiliar venture and exchange offers various advantages, it isn't without its difficulties and intricacies. A portion of the major questions that nations might experience while taking on this approach include:

Financial Disturbance: Abrupt exchange advancement can prompt monetary interruption, especially in businesses that are less serious. Work uprooting and changes in the monetary scene can bring about friendly and political difficulties.

Pay Imbalance: The advantages of unfamiliar venture and exchange may not be uniformly dispersed, possibly compounding pay disparity. Those in trade arranged ventures or high-talented positions might receive more significant benefits, while others might confront deteriorating earnings.

Exchange Uneven characters: Extending exchange can bring about exchange irregular characteristics, where a nation imports more than it sends out. Constant import/export imbalances can prompt money devaluation and financial weaknesses.

Ecological Worries: Expanded financial movement, especially in asset serious ventures, can have negative natural outcomes. Nations might confront difficulties in offsetting financial development with natural supportability.

Protectionist Measures: Unfamiliar venture and exchange can be ruined by protectionist measures forced by exchanging accomplices, like duties, non-levy hindrances, and exchange debates.

Loss of Homegrown Control: Opening up to unfamiliar speculation can prompt worries about the deficiency of command over homegrown enterprises, assets, and key resources. Unfamiliar proprietorship in key areas might raise issues of public safety.

Political and Administrative Difficulties: Contrasts in political and administrative structures between nations can present difficulties for organizations and financial backers. Errors in overall sets of laws, property freedoms security, and agreement authorization might make vulnerabilities.

Reliance on Worldwide Business sectors: An inordinate reliance on worldwide business sectors can make nations powerless against outside monetary shocks and market changes, as seen during the worldwide monetary emergency of 2008.

Social and Social Effect: Unfamiliar venture and exchange can achieve social and social changes. The reception of unfamiliar practices and the convergence of global partnerships can have suggestions for neighborhood societies and customs.

International Strains: The convergence of unfamiliar venture and international affairs can some of the time lead to pressures or clashes. Political questions or endorses can upset exchange and speculation streams.

Strategy Decisions and Contemplations

Nations considering opening up to unfamiliar speculation and exchange should cautiously gauge the approach decisions and contemplations associated with the cycle. Key contemplations include:

Sequencing and Timing: Choosing when and how to open up to unfamiliar venture and exchange is critical. Policymakers need to consider the sequencing of changes and the planning of their execution to limit disturbances.

Administrative System: Fostering a straightforward and unsurprising administrative structure is fundamental to draw in unfamiliar financial backers and merchants. Clear standards and guidelines can decrease dangers and vulnerabilities.

Institutional Limit: Compelling organizations that authorize property privileges, safeguard agreements, and resolve questions are crucial for cultivating trust and certainty among unfamiliar financial backers and exchanging accomplices.

Framework Improvement: Interest in foundation, like transportation and operations, can work on the network and seriousness of a country in the worldwide market.

Abilities and Training: Fostering a gifted and taught labor force is fundamental to guarantee that a nation can profit from unfamiliar venture and exchange by successfully partaking in worldwide worth chains.

Wellbeing Nets and Social Insurance: Tending to pay imbalance and social abberations might require the execution of security nets and social assurance projects to help weak sections of the populace.

Maintainability and Natural Contemplations: Offsetting monetary development with ecological supportability is a basic test. Nations need to foster techniques and strategies that address natural worries and advance feasible practices.

Broadening and Chance Administration: Policymakers ought to consider enhancing the country's monetary base and carrying out risk the executives techniques to relieve possible financial weaknesses.

6.3 The impact on Indian industry and economy

The opening up of the Indian economy to unfamiliar speculation and exchange, especially through the monetary changes of 1991, significantly affects the country's business and economy. This effect incorporates many monetary areas, strategy changes, and cultural changes. India's excursion towards globalization has prompted the two open doors and difficulties, with impacts felt across different aspects, from assembling and administrations to advancement and occupation creation. This paper investigates the multi-layered influence on Indian industry and economy, revealing insight into the massive changes and intricacies achieved by the country's financial progression and mix into the worldwide economy.

Fabricating and Modern Development

The progression of India's economy, including decreased exchange hindrances, exchange strategy changes, and a more noteworthy accentuation on trade situated development, has fundamentally impacted the nation's assembling area. Key improvements include:

Auto Industry: The auto area has encountered exceptional development, drawing in worldwide makers and prompting the creation of top notch vehicles. Global joint efforts and ventures have brought about creative and innovatively progressed items.

Drugs: India's drug industry has turned into a worldwide pioneer, providing superior grade, minimal expense meds to both homegrown and global business sectors. The area's development is a demonstration of India's assembling capacities and innovative work exercises.

Materials and Pieces of clothing: Material and piece of clothing producing has extended, with India turning into a central part in the worldwide style and clothing industry. Further developed foundation and admittance to worldwide business sectors have worked with commodities of material and attire items.

Data Innovation (IT) Equipment: The IT equipment industry has grown essentially, with India arising as a producer of PC equipment and peripherals. Government motivations have helped the area's development.

Hardware Assembling: The "Make in India" drive, sent off in 2014, planned to advance gadgets producing in the country. It has prompted expanded speculations and the foundation of gadgets producing center points.

Synthetic compounds and Petrochemicals: The synthetic substances and petrochemicals area has seen extension, driven by request from different ventures, including farming, development, and buyer products.

These improvements have added to modern development and development, making India a worldwide assembling center point. Nonetheless, there have additionally been difficulties, including natural worries, work issues, and the requirement for additional framework advancement.

Administrations Area Headway

India's administrations area has gone through a noteworthy change in the time of globalization, especially determined by the IT and business process rethinking (BPO) industry. Central issues include:

IT and Programming Administrations: India's IT and programming administrations area has turned into a worldwide pioneer, offering many administrations, from programming improvement and support to framework incorporation and counseling. The area has drawn in unfamiliar speculation and made huge number of occupations.

Business Cycle Reevaluating (BPO): India has turned into a favored objective for worldwide organizations trying to re-appropriate different administrations, including client service, administrative center tasks, and money and bookkeeping. The BPO business plays had a critical impact in work creation and monetary development.

Programming Product: The country's product send out incomes have developed fundamentally, making India one of the world's driving programming exporters.

Broadcast communications and Media: The broadcast communications and media areas have encountered development, with the multiplication of portable administrations and satellite TV. These areas have achieved better network and extended admittance to data.

The travel industry: The travel industry area has developed, drawing in guests from around the world. Further developed foundation and advertising endeavors have helped the country's travel industry.

The administrations area's prosperity has brought about an expanded portion of Gross domestic product, work amazing open doors, and the improvement of particular abilities. India's informed labor force, capability in English, and financially savvy work play had a crucial impact in making the country a favored objective for worldwide administrations.

Advancement and Innovative Trade

The course of globalization and expanded unfamiliar speculation has worked with the exchange of innovation and information to India. This trade has brought about prominent turns of events, including:

Innovative work (Research and development): Worldwide enterprises (MNCs) working in India have laid out Research and development focuses, driving mechanical headways and advancement. These focuses have zeroed in on item advancement, process improvement, and statistical surveying.

New businesses and Business venture: The enterprising biological system in India has prospered, with a flood in new companies across different areas. Unfamiliar speculations, investment, and private backers have given financing and backing to development.

Schooling and Expertise Advancement: Admittance to worldwide data, online courses, and instructive assets has further developed training and ability improvement. India has turned into a center point for Itself and programming related schooling and preparing.

Innovation Move: Joint effort with unfamiliar accomplices has worked with the exchange of innovation across areas, from drugs to data innovation and sustainable power.

The trading of information and innovation plays had an essential impact in supporting India's development capacities and improving its upper hand in different businesses.

Work Creation and Business Open doors

One of the critical effects of India's globalization process has been the formation of work open doors. Central issues include:

IT and BPO Area: The IT and BPO industry has produced large number of immediate and aberrant positions. It has been a significant wellspring of work for the nation's informed youth.

Fabricating: The development of assembling areas, for example, auto and materials, has prompted work creation in both metropolitan and provincial regions.

Administrations: The extension of the administrations area has brought about an extensive variety of open positions, from client service jobs to programming improvement and information examination.

Business venture: The ascent of new companies and business has urged people to make their organizations, adding to work creation and monetary dynamism.

Development and Framework: Foundation improvement projects have given positions in the development area, from building streets and extensions to creating savvy urban communities.

Work creation essentially affects decreasing joblessness and working on expectations for everyday comforts. Nonetheless, challenges stay, for example, guaranteeing quality work, tending to underemployment, and dealing with the expertise hole.

Trade Open doors and Admittance to Worldwide Business sectors

India's receptiveness to unfamiliar speculation and exchange has extended trade open doors and further developed admittance to worldwide business sectors. Key improvements include:

Trade Development: India's products have developed, helping different areas, including assembling, administrations, and farming. Commodities of labor and products have turned into a critical driver of financial development.

Expansion of Commodities: India has expanded its product base, with an emphasis on data innovation, drugs, materials, designing merchandise, and farming items.

Worldwide Stock Chains: India has turned into a basic piece of worldwide stockpile chains, taking part in the assembling and appropriation of items across the world.

Unfamiliar Market Access: Admittance to worldwide business sectors has empowered Indian organizations to extend their client base and enter new business sectors, adding to business development and benefit.

Monetary Strategy: The Indian government has effectively participated in financial discretion, producing economic alliance, and associations with nations and locales to help exchange and venture.

The extension of commodities and admittance to worldwide business sectors have upgraded monetary development and given open doors to organizations, everything being equal. India's vigorous programming and IT administrations trades, specifically, play had a critical impact in situating the country on the worldwide financial guide.

Difficulties and Intricacies

While India's excursion towards globalization has achieved various advantages, it has additionally raised a few difficulties and intricacies:

Pay Imbalance: The advantages of globalization have not been equitably conveyed, prompting pay disparity. Those in trade situated ventures or high-gifted positions will quite often receive more significant benefits, while others might confront deteriorating livelihoods.

Social Government assistance and Disparity: The quest for financial advancement now and again came to the detriment of social government assistance. Lacking wellbeing nets and restricted admittance to medical care and training have allowed weak populaces to stay uncovered to monetary shocks.

Ecological Maintainability: Quick industrialization, expanded energy utilization, and urbanization have presented ecological difficulties, including air and water contamination, deforestation, and the exhaustion of normal assets.

Administrative Difficulties: While progression meant to lessen unofficial laws, it has likewise uncovered administrative difficulties in different areas, including medical services, ecological security, and work regulations.

Political and International Intricacies: India's commitment with the worldwide economy has presented new elements of political and international intricacies. The nation should explore worldwide exchange discussions, licensed innovation privileges issues, and conciliatory difficulties connected with monetary associations.

Instruction and Expertise Improvement: The development of the IT and administrations area has highlighted the requirement for a talented labor force. India faces the test of improving its schooling and ability advancement frameworks .

Chapter 7

"Entrepreneurial Spirit: Success Stories and Challenges"

The innovative soul is a main impetus that has molded our reality for quite a long time. It's a persistent craving to make, develop, and immediately jump all over chances chasing achievement. This soul has prompted probably the most astounding accomplishments ever, from the innovation of the light to the establishing of tech monsters like Apple and Google. Yet, in addition to the examples of overcoming adversity characterize the pioneering soul; it's likewise the endless difficulties and mishaps that business visionaries face en route. In this paper, we will investigate the enterprising soul from a perspective that envelops both examples of overcoming adversity and the obstacles that business people experience on their excursion.

Examples of overcoming adversity

The enterprising soul is frequently connected with momentous developments and wonderful examples of overcoming adversity. These stories of win motivate people to face challenges and leave on their own pioneering ventures. One of the most notable examples of overcoming adversity is that of Thomas Edison, the creator of the light. Edison's tenacious quest for a functional electric light source influenced the world, enlightening homes, roads, and urban communities. His assurance to explore different avenues regarding incalculable materials and plans until he accomplished a functioning light is a demonstration of the force of the enterprising soul.

In the domain of innovation, Apple Inc. remains as a demonstration of the pioneering soul. Established by Steve Occupations, Steve Wozniak, and Ronald Wayne in a carport, the organization developed to become one of the world's most important and powerful innovation goliaths. Occupations' vision and tireless quest for flawlessness prompted the making of notorious items like the iPhone, iPad, and MacBook. Apple's prosperity grandstands the force of vision and development when driven by areas of strength for a soul.

Likewise, the ascent of Google is a current example of overcoming adversity that embodies the enterprising soul. Larry Page and Sergey Brin began their excursion in a Stanford College apartment, and their web crawler changed how data is gotten to. Today, Google isn't just a predominant web search tool yet additionally a key part in different tech-related fields, like man-made reasoning and self-driving vehicles. Page and Brin's capacity to distinguish open doors and adjust to the developing tech scene highlights the substance of business.

Another outstanding example of overcoming adversity is that of Elon Musk. Musk helped to establish PayPal and afterward happened to establish SpaceX, Tesla, and SolarCity. His undertakings in space investigation, electric vehicles, and sustainable power have reclassified enterprises. Musk's desire and capacity to handle bold objectives feature how the enterprising soul can drive people to make a critical effect on the world.

Challenges

While examples of overcoming adversity act as persuasive benchmarks, the way of business is frequently loaded with difficulties and hindrances. These hardships are essential to the innovative excursion and shape the personality of the individuals who leave on it.

One of the essential difficulties business people face is getting supporting for their endeavors. Beginning a business, fostering an item, or sending off another undertaking frequently requires a significant measure of capital. Business people might have to look for subsidizing from financial backers, investors, or secure advances from monetary establishments. The method involved with trying out thoughts, arranging terms, and getting financing can be an overwhelming errand, as financial backers are regularly risk-unwilling and search for areas of strength for an arrangement and a make way to productivity.

Notwithstanding monetary difficulties, business visionaries frequently experience administrative obstacles. Exploring the complicated snare of regulations and guidelines, particularly in vigorously controlled enterprises like medical services or money, can be a tedious and expensive undertaking. Consistence with these guidelines is fundamental to stay away from lawful issues that could compromise the feasibility of the business.

Market rivalry is another critical test. In the present globalized world, business people should fight with laid out contenders and new contestants in their separate ventures. Fostering an extraordinary incentive and separating one's item or administration from the opposition is a steady battle. Business people should persistently improve to remain on top of things.

Business is intrinsically dangerous, and business visionaries should be ready to confront disappointment. Few out of every odd thought or business will succeed, and misfortunes are an inescapable piece of the excursion. Managing disappointment can be sincerely and monetarily depleting, and it takes a strong soul to get the pieces and begin once more.

Building an able group is a test that can't be put into words. As a business develops, it becomes critical to gather a capable and devoted labor force. Finding the ideal people who share the pioneering vision and are focused on the mission can be an overwhelming undertaking. Keeping up with group union and inspiration is a continuous test as the association advances.

The questionable and erratic nature of business can likewise negatively affect balance between fun and serious activities. Business people frequently end up working extended periods of time and making individual penances to keep their endeavors above water. Adjusting the requests of a business with individual life can be a steady battle.

The mental cost of business venture ought to be acknowledged with a sober mind. The strain to succeed, go with basic choices, and deal with the business' highs and lows can prompt pressure, nervousness, and burnout. Emotional wellness is a basic worry that business visionaries should address to keep up with their prosperity.

Beating Difficulties

Regardless of the various difficulties, numerous business visionaries have effectively explored the innovative scene. They have taken on procedures and ways to deal with beat impediments and accomplish their objectives.

One of the vital systems for defeating difficulties is compelling preparation and chance administration. A thoroughly examined strategy that expects likely detours and diagrams moderation techniques can give a guide to progress. Business visionaries ought to likewise foster a monetary arrangement that records for different situations and guarantees the manageability of the business.

Looking for mentorship and counsel from experienced business visionaries can be priceless. Gaining from the people who have confronted comparative difficulties and won can give important bits of knowledge and direction. Mentorship programs and systems administration occasions offer chances to interface with prepared business people who can offer counsel and backing.

Flexibility is a critical quality for business visionaries. In a quickly changing business climate, the capacity to turn and change methodologies is fundamental. Business people ought to ceaselessly survey their plans of action and take an alternate route when fundamental. This adaptability can assist them with remaining cutthroat and applicable.

Joint effort and associations can likewise be instrumental in defeating difficulties. Business people can use the qualities and assets of others to resolve normal issues. Cooperative endeavors can prompt creative arrangements and shared triumphs.

Business visionaries ought to focus on taking care of oneself and prosperity. Keeping a solid balance between serious and fun activities, looking for help from loved ones, and tending to emotional well-being concerns are fundamental for long haul achievement. A strong outlook and the capacity to return from difficulties are imperative for persevering through the difficulties of business venture.

Government strategies and support projects can assume a part in facilitating the pioneering venture. Admittance to subsidizing, charge impetuses, and administrative rearrangements can make it more straightforward for business people to explore the business scene. Policymakers can empower business by establishing a climate that cultivates advancement and chance taking.

The Job of Schooling

Schooling and preparing are basic components in supporting the enterprising soul. Business programs in colleges and professional foundations give hopeful business visionaries the information and abilities expected to explore the mind boggling business world. These projects offer seminars on business arranging, showcasing, money, and advancement.

Besides, business venture instruction urges understudies to foster an outlook that embraces risk, cultivates inventiveness, and values critical thinking. Understudies are urged to think fundamentally, distinguish valuable open doors, and develop a pioneering mentality. These abilities are adaptable and can be applied to different parts of life and work.

Numerous fruitful business people acknowledge their schooling as a critical consider their prosperity. Securing information, building organizations, and acquiring openness to true difficulties can give hopeful business people an early advantage on their pioneering venture.

Government Drives and Arrangements

Legislatures all over the planet perceive the significance of business in encouraging financial development and advancement. Accordingly, they frequently carry out approaches and drives to help and energize business venture.

One of the critical areas of government support is admittance to subsidizing. States might give awards, low-interest advances, or assessment motivators to business visionaries and new companies. These monetary motivating forces can assist business visionaries with getting the capital expected to send off their organizations or foster new items.

Notwithstanding monetary help, legislatures might offer mentorship and warning projects. These projects associate business people with experienced tutors who can give direction and backing. Such mentorship can be priceless in assisting business visionaries with exploring the difficulties of beginning and maintaining a business.

Decreasing administrative weights is another way legislatures can advance business venture. Working on the most common way of beginning and working a business can urge more people to seek after innovative endeavors. Smoothed out guidelines, business-accommodating approaches, and computerized stages for enrollments and consistence can fundamentally .

7.1 Profiles of successful Indian entrepreneurs

India, a country famous for its rich history and different culture, has likewise arisen as a hotbed for pioneering ability throughout the long term. The pioneering soul in

India has led to a large number of visionary pioneers who have reformed their particular ventures as well as left an enduring engraving on the worldwide business scene. In this investigation of fruitful Indian business visionaries, we dive into the tales of a few people who have accomplished striking accomplishments, exhibiting their strength, development, and capacity to transform dreams into the real world.

Mukesh Ambani

Mukesh Ambani, the Administrator and Overseeing Head of Dependence Businesses Restricted (RIL), is quite possibly of India's most noticeable and effective business visionary. Brought into the world in Yemen in 1957, Mukesh Ambani hails from the powerful Ambani family, which plays had a vital impact in India's business scene. Under Mukesh's initiative, RIL has developed from a material business to an expanded combination with interests in petrochemicals, refining, broadcast communications, retail, and computerized administrations.

Mukesh Ambani's example of overcoming adversity is a demonstration of his visionary methodology and persevering quest for development. One of his most critical commitments to the Indian business world has been the send off of Dependence Jio Infocomm, a broadcast communications organization that upset the business by offering reasonable information benefits and changing the manner in which Indians access the web. This problematic methodology not just changed the elements of the telecom area yet in addition affected different businesses, like web based business, diversion, and computerized administrations.

Ambani's enterprising excursion has not been without challenges. The media communications area in India is profoundly aggressive and dependent upon huge administrative oversight. Notwithstanding, his enduring obligation to giving available and reasonable advanced administrations to all Indians has pushed him to the bleeding edge of the business.

Notwithstanding his commitments to the business world, Mukesh Ambani is perceived for his generous undertakings, zeroing in on medical services, schooling, and provincial turn of events. His example of overcoming adversity highlights the effect that a visionary business person can have on society overall.

Ratan Goodbye

Ratan Maritime Goodbye, the previous Executive of Goodbye Children, one of India's biggest and most seasoned aggregates, is a notable figure in the Indian business scene. Brought into the world in 1937, Ratan Goodbye assumed control over the Goodbye Gathering in 1991, and during his residency, he changed the association into a worldwide force to be reckoned with interests in different areas, including steel, cars, data innovation, and friendliness.

One of Ratan Goodbye's most imperative accomplishments was the procurement of Panther Land Meanderer, a move that impelled Goodbye Engines onto the worldwide stage. This essential choice displayed his capacity to recognize potential open doors and go ahead with reasonable plans of action. Notwithstanding beginning suspicion, Goodbye's authority prompted the restoration and outcome of these notorious English car brands.

Notwithstanding his commitments to the business world, Ratan Goodbye is known for his charitable undertakings. He laid out the Goodbye Trusts, which center around different social and philanthropic causes, including medical care, schooling, and rustic turn of events. His obligation to rewarding society highlights the significance of corporate social obligation in the realm of business.

Azim Premji

Azim Hashim Premji, the Executive of Wipro Restricted, is prestigious for his enterprising accomplishment as well as for his wonderful excursion of charity. Brought into the world in 1945, Premji acquired a little cooking oil business from his dad in 1966. Nonetheless, his pioneering soul drove him to change it into one of India's driving data innovation organizations, Wipro.

Under Premji's initiative, Wipro expanded into programming administrations, data innovation counseling, and business process re-appropriating. His capacity to adjust to changing business sector elements and reliably convey quality administrations empowered Wipro to set up a good foundation for itself as a worldwide IT administrations supplier.

What separates Azim Premji is his remarkable obligation to altruism. In 2001, he established the Azim Premji Establishment, which centers around further developing schooling and proficiency in India. He swore a huge piece of his abundance to the establishment, underscoring the significance of rewarding society. Premji's commitment to social causes exhibits the potential for business people to have a beneficial outcome on society through both business achievement and charity.

Narayana Murthy

Nagavara Ramarao Narayana Murthy, frequently alluded to as N. R. Narayana Murthy, is the prime supporter of Infosys, one of India's most conspicuous and fruitful data innovation organizations. Brought into the world in 1946, Narayana Murthy's excursion as a business person is a demonstration of his vision, administration, and devotion to quality.

Narayana Murthy and six other prime supporters began Infosys in 1981 with a dream to make a worldwide innovation administrations organization. Under his authority, Infosys turned into a trailblazer in the Indian IT industry, giving programming counseling and IT administrations to clients around the world. The organization's obligation to greatness and moral strategic policies put it aside and established the groundwork for its worldwide achievement.

Narayana Murthy's innovative excursion has been set apart by a pledge to corporate administration, straightforwardness, and a solid accentuation on friendly obligation. He has been a vocal supporter for corporate morals and uprightness, and these qualities have been vital to Infosys' way of life. His authority at Infosys and his commitments to the IT business have made him a regarded figure in both business and generosity.

Kiran Mazumdar-Shaw

Kiran Mazumdar-Shaw, the Executive and Overseeing Overseer of Biocon Restricted, is a pioneer in the area of biotechnology and drugs. Brought into the world in 1953, she is frequently alluded to as the "Biotech Sovereign of India" and has made critical commitments to the Indian medical services industry.

Mazumdar-Shaw established Biocon in 1978, when the biotechnology business in India was still in its earliest stages. Her pioneering venture was set apart by various difficulties, including getting subsidizing and exploring complex administrative cycles. In spite of these obstacles, she drove forward and incorporated Biocon into a main biotechnology organization with a worldwide impression.

Biocon has some expertise in biopharmaceuticals, including insulin and other biologic items, and assumes a urgent part in tending to medical services difficulties in India and then some. Mazumdar-Shaw's devotion to advancement, exploration, and quality has been instrumental in Biocon's prosperity.

Past her innovative accomplishments, Kiran Mazumdar-Shaw is a defender of corporate social obligation and reasonable strategic policies. She has been a vocal backer for reasonable medical services and has been engaged with different magnanimous drives, especially in the space of medical services and training.

Shiv Nadar

Shiv Nadar, the organizer behind HCL (Hindustan PCs Restricted), is a trailblazer in the Indian data innovation industry. Brought into the world in 1945, Nadar's enterprising excursion started in the last part of the 1970s when he helped to establish HCL with a dream to foster the native PC equipment industry in India.

Under Nadar's authority, HCL became one of India's driving IT administrations organizations, giving programming administrations, equipment arrangements, and innovation counseling. The organization's obligation to development and quality prompted its development as a worldwide IT player.

Shiv Nadar's innovative achievement is a consequence of his capacity to recognize market open doors and adjust to changing innovation scenes. His vision stretched out past business, as he laid out the Shiv Nadar Establishment, which centers around schooling and workmanship. The establishment means to advance greatness in training and support imaginative ability in India, stressing the significance of magnanimity in sustaining the fate of the country.

Kiran Mazumdar-Shaw, the Executive and Overseeing Overseer of Biocon Restricted, is a pioneer in the area of biotechnology and drugs. Brought into the world in 1953, she is frequently alluded to as the "Biotech Sovereign of India" and has made critical commitments to the Indian medical care industry.

Mazumdar-Shaw established Biocon in 1978, when the biotechnology business in India was still in its early stages. Her enterprising excursion was set apart by various difficulties, including getting subsidizing and exploring complex administrative cycles. Notwithstanding these obstacles, she drove forward and incorporated Biocon into a main biotechnology organization with a worldwide impression.

Biocon has some expertise in biopharmaceuticals, including insulin and other biologic items, and assumes a critical part in tending to medical care difficulties in India and then some. Mazumdar-Shaw's devotion to advancement, examination, and quality has been instrumental in Biocon's prosperity.

Past her innovative accomplishments, Kiran Mazumdar-Shaw is a defender of corporate social obligation and reasonable strategic policies. She has been a vocal promoter for reasonable medical care and has been engaged with different charitable drives, especially in the space of medical services and schooling.

Shiv Nadar

Shiv Nadar, the organizer behind HCL (Hindustan PCs Restricted), is a trailblazer in the Indian data innovation industry. Brought into the world in 1945, Nadar's pioneering venture started in the last part of the 1970s when he helped to establish HCL with a dream to foster the native PC equipment industry in India.

Under Nadar's authority, HCL became one of India's driving IT administrations organizations, giving programming administrations, equipment arrangements, and innovation counseling. The organization's obligation to development and quality prompted its development as a worldwide IT player.

7.2 Challenges faced by entrepreneurs in a competitive global market

The enterprising excursion is set apart by aspiration, development, and the quest for a potential open door. Business visionaries frequently endeavor to transform their imaginative thoughts into feasible organizations that can flourish in an undeniably aggressive worldwide market. In any case, this way is full of difficulties that require creativity, strength, and versatility. In this investigation of the difficulties looked by business people in the present worldwide market, we dig into the diverse obstructions that can impede the development and outcome of pioneering adventures.

Wild Contest: The worldwide market is profoundly cutthroat, with innumerable players competing for piece of the pie. New business visionaries frequently wind up facing laid out goliaths with broad assets and market presence. Rivaling industry pioneers can be overwhelming, and hanging out in a packed commercial center is a huge test.

Admittance to Capital: Getting financing is really difficult for business people. While there are different wellsprings of capital, like investment, private backers, and conventional bank credits, accessing these assets can challenge. Financial backers are many times risk-unwilling and look for convincing strategies and strong monetary projections, which can be challenging for new businesses to give.

Statistical surveying and Understanding: Business people need to completely comprehend their objective business sectors. Leading extensive statistical surveying is fundamental for recognizing client needs, inclinations, and ways of behaving. This is vital for making items or administrations that fulfill market needs. Without precise market bits of knowledge, business people risk creating items that have no market fit.

Administrative and Lawful Obstacles: Exploring the mind boggling snare of guidelines and legitimate prerequisites can be difficult for business people. Various businesses and locales have their own principles and consistence norms that business people should stick to. Administrative difficulties can make delays, inflate expenses, and even lead to legitimate issues that can compromise the practicality of the business.

Worldwide Extension and Limitation: Extending a business internationally is a critical achievement for business people, however it accompanies a one of a kind arrangement of difficulties. Business people should adjust to various societies, dialects, and lawful systems. Scaling a business in another nation or district requires market information as well as successful restriction and circulation methodologies.

Store network The executives: The proficient administration of the store network is fundamental for some organizations. Guaranteeing a reliable stockpile of unrefined components and opportune conveyance of items to clients is an intricate interaction that can be upset by unexpected occasions, like catastrophic events, international issues, or transportation interruptions.

Ability Obtaining and Maintenance: Building a talented and persuaded group is basic for business achievement. Drawing in and holding top ability is difficult for business people, as they frequently contend with bigger organizations that can offer more significant compensations and more extensive advantages. Making a convincing work environment culture and offering potential open doors for vocation development is fundamental in tending to this test.

Advertising and Marking: Successful showcasing and brand-building are fundamental to making mindfulness and drawing in clients. Business people should beat the test of building areas of strength for a personality and arriving at their ideal interest group in a savvy way. The quickly developing computerized scene adds intricacy to showcasing endeavors.

Changing Shopper Conduct: Buyer conduct is continually developing, impacted by variables like innovative headways, monetary changes, and cultural patterns. Business people should adjust to these movements to stay important and meet the changing requirements and inclinations of their clients.

Licensed innovation Security: Safeguarding licensed innovation is urgent for some business visionaries, particularly those in innovation, imaginative, or creative ventures. Licenses, brand names, and copyrights are imperative resources that require lawful security. Licensed innovation burglary and encroachment can present critical dangers.

Network safety Dangers: With expanding digitalization, business visionaries are presented to online protection dangers that can think twice about information and harm the standing of their organizations. Executing powerful network protection measures to defend client data and business tasks is a squeezing concern.

Maintainability and Ecological Obligation: Tending to natural difficulties, including environmental change and asset exhaustion, has turned into a need for organizations. Business visionaries are progressively expected to integrate maintainable practices into their tasks, which can be both a test and a chance for separation.

Monetary Unpredictability: Worldwide financial circumstances, including market vacillations, expansion, and international shakiness, can essentially influence business tasks. Business people should foster monetary procedures to endure financial unpredictability and adjust to changing financial scenes.

Developing Innovation: Remaining refreshed with quickly developing innovation is quite difficult for business visionaries. Innovation can both upset and improve business activities, and business visionaries need to embrace developments to remain cutthroat.

Quick Market Changes: Markets can change quickly, and business people should be deft in answering changes sought after, arising patterns, and cutthroat tensions. Inability to adjust to advertise changes can prompt outdated nature.

Brand Notoriety The executives: A business' standing is a significant resource, and overseeing it successfully is fundamental. Negative exposure or advertising issues can hurt a brand's picture and effect client trust. Business people need to foster emergency the executives and notoriety fix methodologies.

Scaling and Development: As organizations develop, they experience difficulties connected with scaling activities, keeping up with quality, and holding the spryness that at first drove their prosperity. Dealing with this development successfully is a fragile difficult exercise for business visionaries.

Globalization and International Dangers: International occasions, for example, exchange debates and political shakiness, can affect worldwide business tasks. Business visionaries took part in worldwide business sectors should explore these dangers while looking for valuable learning experiences.

Computerized Change: Embracing advanced change is urgent in the present business climate. Business people should put resources into innovation to smooth out tasks, upgrade client encounters, and stay cutthroat in a computerized world.

Client Maintenance and Steadfastness: Procuring new clients is regularly more costly than holding existing ones. Business visionaries should zero in on areas of strength for building connections and dedication projects to guarantee rehash business.

Tending to these difficulties requires a blend of key preparation, versatility, a pledge to development, and a readiness to gain from disappointments. Effective business visionaries comprehend that provokes are not barricades but rather chances to improve and develop. By tending to these deterrents head-on, business people can upgrade their possibilities flourishing in the serious worldwide market.

7.3 The spirit of Indian entrepreneurship

India, a place where there is different societies, dialects, and customs, has a rich history of business venture that goes back millennia. The soul of Indian business venture has persevered through various ages, from the antiquated shipping lanes that associated India to the remainder of the world to the contemporary tech new companies that have transformed the worldwide stage. This article investigates the pith of Indian business, enveloping its verifiable roots, challenges, and the unique environment that portrays the pioneering scene in India today.

Verifiable Foundations of Indian Business venture

The pioneering soul in India can be followed back to old times when the subcontinent was known for its lively exchange with districts like the Center East, Southeast Asia, and Europe. Indian vendors assumed a significant part in these exchange organizations, moving merchandise, information, and culture across huge distances.

The renowned Silk Street, an organization of shipping lanes interfacing Asia to Europe, was fundamental to these trades. Merchants from India, known as "Saraf" in Persian, were exceptionally respected for their abilities and honesty.

India's set of experiences is additionally set apart by flourishing metropolitan places and exchange centers, for example, the antiquated city of Varanasi, which goes back north of 2,500 years. These urban areas were focuses of business and advancement, drawing in traders and business people from all over.

The Mughal Domain (sixteenth to eighteenth hundreds of years) further added to the pioneering soul in India. It encouraged a prospering economy and a different scope of business visionaries, including brokers, craftsmans, and talented experts. The Mughals laid out complicated frameworks of business, which impacted Indian exchange and enterprising practices for quite a long time.

The pilgrim time frame under English rule significantly affected Indian business venture. While English colonization unfavorably affected India's economy, it likewise energized a patriot and pioneering soul that assumed a critical part in the battle for freedom. Mahatma Gandhi's accentuation on independence, or "Swadeshi," urged Indians to help nearby ventures and business. This soul of confidence was an impetus for the improvement of native organizations and a fundamental antecedent to India's post-freedom innovative scene.

Challenges Looked by Indian Business people

Indian business people, similar to their partners all over the planet, stand up to a large number of moves in their excursion to make effective organizations. These moves can be both one of a kind to India and imparted to the worldwide pioneering local area. Here are a portion of the key obstructions looked by Indian business people:

Admittance to Capital: Getting financing stays a critical test for Indian business visionaries. While India has a developing biological system of funding, private supporters, and government drives, getting to capital can be an impressive obstacle, especially for beginning phase new businesses. Financial backers frequently look for a hearty field-tested strategy and a demonstrated history, making it trying for beginner business visionaries.

Organization and Administrative Intricacy: Exploring India's regulatory scene and complex administrative climate can be an overwhelming errand. Business people frequently experience a snare of grants, licenses, and consistence prerequisites that can be tedious and expensive to explore. Improving on these cycles is crucial for encouraging business.

Market Contest: India's immense and different market is portrayed by furious rivalry. Business people need to battle with both neighborhood and worldwide players, making separation and development vital for progress. Arising innovations and changing shopper inclinations additionally heighten contest.

Foundation and Strategies: India's framework and coordinated factors difficulties, including transportation, store network the board, and circulation, can thwart the smooth activity of organizations. Framework enhancements are pivotal to guaranteeing that business people can productively arrive at their clients.

Ability Obtaining and Maintenance: Building a talented labor force is fundamental for the progress of any business. Drawing in and holding top ability in India's serious work market can be testing, particularly for new businesses that will most likely be unable to extend to similar advantages and employment opportunity security as laid out organizations.

Protected innovation Assurance: Defending protected innovation is fundamental for creative organizations. Business people frequently experience difficulties connected with patent recording, brand name enrollment, and safeguarding their developments from burglary or encroachment.

Statistical surveying and Shopper Getting it: Business people need a profound comprehension of their objective business sectors to make items or administrations that address client issues. Directing complete statistical surveying can be tedious and requires assets, which might be scant for new companies.

Computerized Separation: While India is quickly digitizing, there is as yet a critical advanced partition in the country. Business people need to resolve issues connected with computerized admittance, education, and framework to arrive at a wide client base.

Network safety Dangers: With the rising dependence on advanced stages, business people need to safeguard their organizations from online protection dangers. Information breaks and cyberattacks can be annihilating for new businesses and laid out organizations the same.

Social and Semantic Variety: India's social and phonetic variety can present difficulties for organizations hoping to broadly extend. Business visionaries need to adjust their items, promoting procedures, and correspondence to take special care of a different client base.

Market Unpredictability and Monetary Vulnerability: Financial changes and market instability can affect organizations in India. Business people should foster methodologies to climate financial vulnerabilities and acclimate to changing economic situations.

Admittance to Country Markets: While India's metropolitan business sectors are very much served, getting to rustic business sectors presents special difficulties. Business people need creative circulation models to arrive at clients in far off regions.

Natural Obligation: Ecological supportability is an arising challenge for business people. With developing natural mindfulness and administrative changes, organizations need to embrace eco-accommodating practices and add to supportability endeavors.

Emotional well-being and Balance between fun and serious activities: The requests of business venture can negatively affect emotional wellness and balance between fun and serious activities. Business visionaries frequently work extended periods of time and face elevated degrees of stress, making taking care of oneself and psychological wellness support fundamental.

Notwithstanding these difficulties, Indian business people keep on showing strength and assurance, driving financial development and advancement in the country. India's pioneering environment has advanced altogether, offering backing, mentorship, and valuable open doors for new and arising organizations.

The Unique Biological system of Indian Business venture

The enterprising scene in India is portrayed by dynamism and advancement. As of late, the nation has seen a flood in new businesses, especially in areas like innovation, online business, medical services, and money. This enterprising blast has been worked with by different variables that have added to a flourishing environment:

Government Drives: The Indian government has acquainted various drives with advance business, including the "Make in India" mission and "Startup India." These projects expect to improve on administrative cycles, give financing, and backing development.

Hatcheries and Gas pedals: Hatcheries and gas pedals have multiplied the nation over, offering new companies admittance to mentorship, assets, and systems administration valuable open doors. These associations assume a vital part in sustaining new organizations.

Funding and Private supporters: India has seen a development in the funding and private supporter local area. These wellsprings of subsidizing have infused capital into new businesses and furnished them with the monetary help expected to develop.

Enterprising Schooling: Instructive organizations in India are progressively offering business venture projects and encouraging a culture of development. This has prompted a flood in youthful business people with new thoughts and an eagerness to face challenges.

Advancement Centers: Urban areas like Bengaluru, Hyderabad, and Pune have arisen as development center points, drawing in new companies and worldwide organizations the same. These centers offer an energetic biological system with admittance to ability, financial backers, and foundation.

Computerized Change: The advanced change in India has set out new open doors for business people. Admittance to the web, portable innovation, and internet business stages has extended the span of organizations to remote corners of the country.

Social Business: A developing number of business people in India are zeroing in on friendly business. They are utilizing plans of action to resolve social and natural issues, showing a pledge to making a positive effect close by benefits.

Cooperative Biological system: Joint effort is a sign of the Indian enterprising environment. Business visionaries frequently team up with friends, guides, and industry specialists to learn, develop, and address difficulties all things considered.

Worldwide Acknowledgment: Indian new companies have earned respect on the worldwide stage, with many getting ventures and backing from global financial backers and hatcheries. This worldwide openness has opened ways to global business sectors and associations.

New businesses in Specialty Areas: New companies are not restricted to innovation and online business. India has seen business arise in specialty areas like economical agribusiness, medical services innovation, and sustainable power.

The Indian enterprising soul isn't restricted to a particular area or segment; it rises above geological limits and incorporates a different scope of business people. Ladies business visionaries, specifically, have been making critical .